新丝路“中文+职业技能”系列教材
New Silk Road “Chinese + Vocational Skills” Series

中文+计算机网络技术

Chinese + Computer Networking Technology

初级 Elementary

新丝路“中文+职业技能”系列教材编写委员会 编

北京语言大学出版社
BEIJING LANGUAGE AND CULTURE
UNIVERSITY PRESS

图书在版编目（CIP）数据

中文＋计算机网络技术．初级 / 新丝路“中文＋职业技能”系列教材编写委员会编．-- 北京：北京语言大学出版社，2023.9（2025.1 重印）
新丝路“中文＋职业技能”系列教材
ISBN 978-7-5619-6323-4

Ⅰ．①中… Ⅱ．①新… Ⅲ．①汉语－对外汉语教学－教材 ②计算机网络－教材 Ⅳ．① H195.4 ② TP393.08

中国国家版本馆 CIP 数据核字（2023）第 161687 号

中文＋计算机网络技术（初级）

ZHONGWEN + JISUANJI WANGLUO JISHU (CHUJI)

排版制作：北京创艺涵文化发展有限公司
责任印制：周 燚

出版发行：北京语言大学出版社
社 址：北京市海淀区学院路 15 号，100083
网 址：www.blcup.com
电子信箱：service@blcup.com
电 话：编 辑 部 8610-82303647/3592/3395
国内发行 8610-82303650/3591/3648
海外发行 8610-82303365/3080/3668
北语书店 8610-82303653
网购咨询 8610-82303908
印 刷：北京富资园科技发展有限公司

版 次：2023 年 9 月第 1 版　　印 次：2025 年 1 月第 3 次印刷
开 本：889 毫米 × 1194 毫米 1/16　　印 张：10
字 数：189 千字
定 价：98.00 元

PRINTED IN CHINA
凡有印装质量问题，本社负责调换。售后 QQ 号 1367565611，电话 010-82303590

编写说明

新丝路“中文＋职业技能”系列教材是把中文作为第二语言，结合专业和职业的专门用途、职业用途的中文教材，不是专业理论教材，不是一般意义的通用综合中文教材。本系列教材定位为职场生存中文教材、立体式技能型语言教材。教材研发的目标是既要满足学习者一般中文环境下的基本交际需求，又要满足学习者职业学习需求和职场工作需求。它和普通的国际中文教材的区别不在语法，而在词汇的专门化程度，在中文的用途、使用场合、应用范围。目前，专门用途、职业用途的中文教材在语言分类和研究成果上几近空白，本系列教材的成功研发开创了中文学习的新视野、新领域、新方向，将“中文＋职业技能+X等级证书”真正融合，使学习者在学习中文的同时，也可通过实践掌握职业技能，从而获得X等级证书。

适用对象

本系列教材将适用对象定位为双零基础（零语言基础、零技能基础）的来华学习中文和先进技能的长期或者短期进修生，可满足初、中、高各层次专业课程的教学需要。教材亦可供海内外相关的培训课程及“走出去”的中资企业培训本土化员工使用。

结构规模

本系列教材采取专项语言技能与职业技能训练相结合的中文教学及教材编写模式。教材选择当前热门的物流管理、汽车服务工程技术、电子商务、机电一体化、计算机网络技术、酒店管理等六个专业，培养各专业急需急用的技术岗位人才。每个专业教材均包括初、中、高级三册。每一册都配有专业视频教学资源，还附有“视频脚本”“参考答案”等配套资源。

编写理念

本系列教材将词语进行分类，区分普通词语和专业词语，以通用语料为基础，以概念性、行为性词语为主，不脱离职场情境讨论分级，做到控制词汇量，控制工作场景，控制交流内容与方式，构建语义框架。将语言的分级和专业的分级科学地融合，是实现本系列教材成功编写的关键。

教材目标

语言技能目标：

初级阶段，能熟练掌握基础通用词语和职场的常用专业词语，能使用简短句子进行简单的生活及工作交流。中级阶段，能听懂工作场合简单的交谈与发言，明白大意，把握基本情况，能就工作中重要的话题用简单的话与人沟通。高级阶段，能听懂工作场合一般的交谈与发言，抓住主要内容和关键信息，使用基本交际策略与人交流、开展工作，能初步了解与交际活动相关的文化因素，掌握与交际有关的一般文化背景知识，能排除交际时遇到的文化障碍。交际能力层次的递进实现从初级的常规礼节、基本生活及工作的交流能力，到中级的简单的服务流程信息交流能力，最后达到高级的复杂信息的交流和特情处理的能力。

职业技能目标：

以满足岗位需求为目标，将遴选出的当前热门的专业工作岗位分为初、中、高三级。物流管理专业初、中、高级对应的岗位分别是物流员、物流经理、物流总监；汽车服务工程技术专业初、中、高级对应的岗位分别是汽车机电维修工、汽车服务顾问、技术总监；电子商务专业初、中、高级对应的岗位分别是电子商务运营助理、电子商务运营员、电子商务客服；机电一体化专业初、中、高级对应的岗位分别是机电操作工、机电调整工、机电维修工；计算机网络技术专业初、中、高级对应的岗位分别是宽带运维工程师、网络运维专员、网络管理员；酒店管理专业初、中、高级对应的岗位分别是前厅基层接待员、前厅主管、前厅经理。每个专业分解出三十个工作场景 / 任务，学习者在学习后能够全面掌握此岗位的概况及基本程序，实现语言学习和专业操作的双重目标。

编写原则

1. 语言知识技能与专业知识技能并进，满足当前热门的、急需急用的岗位需求。

2. 渐进分化，综合贯通，拆解难点，分而治之。

3. 语言知识与专业知识科学、高效复现，语言技能与专业技能螺旋式上升，职场情境、语义框架、本体输入方式相互配合。

4. 使用大量的图片和视频，实现专业知识和技能呈现形式可视化。

5. 强化专业岗位实操性技能。本系列教材配有专业技术教学的视频，突出展示专业岗位的实操性技能，语言学习难度与技能掌握难度的不匹配可通过实操性强的视频和实训环节来补充。

特色追求

本系列教材从初级最基础的语音知识学习和岗位认知开始，将“中文＋职业技能”融入在工作场景对话中，把工作分解成一个个任务，用图片认知的方式解决专业词语的认知问题，用视频展示的方法解决学习者掌握中文词语与专业技能的不匹配问题，注重技能的实操性，注重“在做中学”。每一单元都设置了“学以致用”板块，目的不仅仅是解决本单元任务的词语认知问题，更是将学习的目标放在“能听”“能用”“能模仿说出”上。我们力争通过大量图片的使用和配套视频的展示，将教材打造成立体式、技能型语言教材，方便学习者能够更好地自主学习。

使用建议

1. 本系列教材每个专业分为初、中、高级三册，每册10单元，初级每单元建议8～10课时完成，中级 10 ～ 12 课时完成，高级 12 ～ 14 课时完成。

2. 教材注释和说明着力于简明扼要，注重实操性，注重听说技能培养，对于教材涉及的语法知识，教师可视情况予以细化和补充。

3. “单元实训”板块可以在课文和语言点学完之后作为课堂练习使用，建议 2 课时完成。教师要带着学习者按照实训步骤一步步完成，实训步骤不要求学习者能够看懂，读懂，重要的是教师要引领操作，实现学习者掌握专业技能的目标。

4. “单元小结”板块是对整个单元关键词语和核心内容的总结，对于这部分内容，教师要进行听说练习，以便更好地帮助学习者了解本单元的核心工作任务。

5. 教师上课时要充分利用教材设计的练习，引导学习者多听多练，听说结合，学做合一。

6. 教师要带着学习者熟练诵读课文，要求学习者把每课的关键词语和句子、课堂用语背诵下来。

特别感谢

感谢教育部中外语言交流合作中心将新丝路“中文 + 职业技能”系列教材列为重点研发项目，为我们教材编写增添了动力和责任感。教材编写委员会负责整套教材的规划、设计与编写协调，并先后召开上百次讨论会，对每册教材的课文编写、体例安排、注释说明、练习设计、图片选择、视频制作等进行全方位的评估、讨论和审定。感谢编写委员会成员和所有编者高度的敬业精神、精益求精的编写态度，以及所投入的热情和精力、付出的心血与智慧。感谢关注本系列教材并贡献宝贵意见的国际中文教育教学界专家和全国各地的同人。

新丝路“中文 + 职业技能”系列教材编写委员会

2023 年 4 月

Compilation Instructions

The New Silk Road "Chinese + Vocational Skills" is a series of Chinese textbooks for specialized and vocational purposes that combine professional and vocational technologies with Chinese as a second language. Instead of being specialized theoretical textbooks, or comprehensive or universal Chinese textbooks in a general sense, this series is intended to be Chinese textbooks for career survival, and three-dimensional skills-based language textbooks. The textbooks are developed with a view to meeting students' basic communication needs in general Chinese environment, and their professional learning needs and workplace demands as well. They are different from ordinary Chinese textbooks for foreigners in the degree of specialization of vocabulary, in the purpose, usage occasion, and application scope of Chinese (not in grammar). At present, Chinese textbooks for specialized and vocational purposes are virtually non-existent in terms of language classification and research results, so the successful development of this series has opened up new horizons, new fields and new directions for Chinese learning, and virtually integrated "Chinese + Vocational Skills + X-Level Certificates", which enables students to practically master vocational skills and obtain X-level certificates while learning Chinese.

Applicable Targets

This series is targeted at long-term or short-term students who come to China to learn Chinese and advanced skills with zero language basis and zero skill basis, which can meet the teaching needs of the elementary, intermediate and advanced specialized courses. This series can also be used for relevant training courses at home and abroad and for Chinese-funded enterprises that "go global" to train local employees.

Structure and Scale

This series adopts a Chinese teaching and textbook compilation model combining special language skills and vocational skills training. The series includes the textbooks for six popular majors such as logistics management, automotive service engineering technology, e-commerce, mechatronics, computer networking technology, and hotel management to cultivate technical talents in urgent need. The textbooks for each major consist of the textbooks at the elementary, intermediate and advanced levels. Each textbook is equipped with professional video teaching resources, and "video scripts", "reference answers" and other supporting resources as well.

Compilation Concept

This series classifies the vocabulary into general vocabulary and specialized vocabulary. Based on the general vocabulary, it focuses on conceptual and behavioral words, not deviating from workplace situations, so as to control the vocabulary, work scenarios and content and means of communication, and build the semantic framework. The scientific integration of language classification and specialty classification is the key to the successful compilation of textbooks.

Textbook Objectives

Language Skill Objectives

For students at the elementary level, they are trained to be familiar with basic general vocabulary and common specialized vocabulary in the workplace, and be able to use short sentences for simple communication in life and at work. For those at the intermediate level, they are trained to understand simple conversations and speeches in the workplace, comprehend the main ideas, grasp the basic situations, and communicate with others in simple words on important topics at work. For those at the advanced level, they are trained to be able to understand general conversations and speeches in the workplace, grasp the main content and key information, use basic communication strategies to communicate with others and carry out the work, have a preliminary understanding of cultural factors related to communication activities, master the general communication-related cultural background knowledge, and overcome cultural barriers encountered during communication. The progression in level of communicative competence helps them to leap forward from routine etiquette, basic communication in life and at work at the elementary level, to simple information exchange of service processes at the intermediate level, and finally to complex information exchange and handling of special circumstances at the advanced level.

Vocational Skill Objectives

To meet job requirements at the elementary, intermediate and advanced levels, the professional positions that are most urgently needed overseas are selected. The positions corresponding to logistics management at the elementary, intermediate and advanced levels are logistics staff, logistics managers and logistics directors; the positions corresponding to automotive service engineering technology at the elementary, intermediate and advanced levels are automotive electromechanical maintenance staff, automotive service consultants and technical directors; the positions corresponding to e-commerce at the elementary, intermediate and advanced levels are electronic operation assistants, e-commerce operators and e-commerce customer service staff; the positions corresponding to mechatronics at the elementary, intermediate and advanced levels are mechanical and electrical operators, mechanical and electrical adjusters, and mechanical and electrical maintenance staff; the positions corresponding to computer networking technology at the elementary, intermediate and advanced levels are broadband operation and maintenance engineers, network operation and maintenance specialists, and network administrators; the positions corresponding to hotel management at the elementary, intermediate and advanced levels are lobby receptionists, lobby supervisors and lobby managers. Through 30 work scenarios/tasks set for each major, learners can fully grasp the general situations and basic procedures of the position after learning, and achieve the dual goals of language learning and professional operation.

Principles of Compilation

1. Language knowledge skills and professional knowledge skills go hand in hand to meet the demands of current popular and urgently needed job positions;

2. It makes progressive differentiation and comprehensive integration, breaking down, dividing and conquering difficult points;

3. Language knowledge and professional knowledge recur scientifically and efficiently, language skills and professional skills spiral upward, and the situational stage, semantic framework, and ontology input methods cooperate with each other;

4. Professional knowledge and skills are visualized, using a lot of pictures and videos;

5. It strengthens the practical skills in professional positions. This series of textbooks is equipped with videos of professional technical training, highlighting the practical skills for professional positions. It addresses the mismatch between the difficulty of language learning and that of mastering skills by supplementing with practical videos and practical training.

Characteristic Pursuit

Starting from the basic phonetic knowledge learning and job cognition at the elementary level, this series integrates "Chinese + Vocational Skills" into the working scene dialogues, breaking down the job into various tasks, solving lexical students' problems by means of picture cognition, solving the problem of the mismatch between students' mastery of Chinese vocabulary and professional skills by means of displaying videos, stressing the practicality of skills, and focusing on "learning by doing". Each unit has a "Practicing What You Have Learnt" module, which not only solves the problem of lexical cognition of this unit, but also takes "being able to comprehend", "being able to use" and "being able to imitate" as the learning objectives. We strive to use a large number of pictures and display supporting videos to build the textbooks into three-dimensional skills-based language teaching materials, so that learners can learn more independently.

Recommendations for Use

1. Each major of this series consists of three volumes at the elementary, intermediate, and advanced levels, with 10 units in each volume. For each unit, it is recommended to be completed in 8-10 class hours at the elementary level, 10-12 class hours at the intermediate level, and 12-14 class hours at the advanced level.

2. The notes and explanations in the textbooks focus on conciseness, practicality, and the training of listening and speaking skills. The grammar knowledge in the textbooks can be detailed and supplemented by teachers as the case may be.

3. "Unit Practical Training" module can be used as a classroom exercise after the texts and language points, preferably to be completed in two class hours. Teachers should guide students to complete the training tasks step by step. Students are not required to read and understand the training steps. It is important that teachers guide students to achieve the goal of mastering professional skills.

4. "Unit Summary" module summarizes the keywords and core content of the entire unit. Through listening and speaking exercises, this part can better help learners understand the core tasks of this unit.

5. Teachers should make full use of the exercises designed in the textbooks during class, and guide students to listen more and practice more, combine listening and speaking, and integrate learning with practice.

6. Teachers should guide students to proficiently read the texts aloud, asking them to recite the keywords, sentences and classroom expressions in each unit.

Acknowledgements

We are grateful to the Center for Language Education and Cooperation of the Ministry of Education for listing the New Silk Road "Chinese + Vocational Skills" series as a key research and development project, which adds motivation and a sense of responsibility to our textbook compilation. The Textbook Compilation Committee is responsible for the planning, design, compilation and coordination of the entire set of textbooks, and has held hundreds of seminars to conduct a comprehensive evaluation, discussion, examination and approval of text compilation, style arrangement, notes and explanations, exercise design, picture selection, and video production of each textbook. We are indebted to the members of the Compilation Committee and all compilers for their professional dedication, unwavering pursuit of perfection in the compilation, as well as their enthusiasm, hard work and wisdom. We are thankful to the experts in international Chinese language education and colleagues from all over the country who have kept a close eye on this series and contributed their valuable opinions.

Compilation Committee of New Silk Road "Chinese + Vocational Skills" Series

April 2023

gǎngwèi jièshào

岗位介绍

Characters Introduction

wǎngluò gōngchéngshī

网络工程师

Network Engineer

wǎngyè shèjìshī

网页设计师

Web Designer

wǎngzhàn wéihùyuán

网站 维护员

Website Maintainer

jìsuànjī xìtǒng wéihùyuán

计算机系统维护员

Computer System Maintainer

shùjùkù guǎnlǐ yǔ wéihù gōngchéngshī

数据库管理与维护工程师

Database Management & Maintenance Engineer

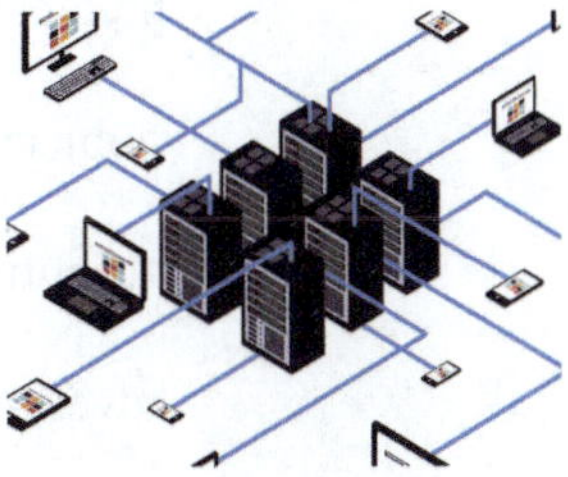

语法术语及缩略形式参照表
Abbreviations of Grammar Terms

Grammar-Terms in Chinese	Grammar-Terms in *Pinyin*	Grammar-Terms in English	Abbreviations
名词	míngcí	noun	n.
专有名词	zhuānyǒu míngcí	proper noun	pn.
代词	dàicí	pronoun	pron.
数词	shùcí	numeral	num.
量词	liàngcí	measure word	m.
数量词	shùliàngcí	quantifier	q.
动词	dòngcí	verb	v.
助动词	zhùdòngcí	auxiliary	aux.
形容词	xíngróngcí	adjective	adj.
副词	fùcí	adverb	adv.
介词	jiècí	preposition	prep.
连词	liáncí	conjunction	conj.
助词	zhùcí	particle	part.
拟声词	nǐshēngcí	onomatopoeia	onom.
叹词	tàncí	interjection	int.
前缀	qiánzhuì	prefix	pref.
后缀	hòuzhuì	suffix	suf.
成语	chéngyǔ	idiom	idm.
短语	duǎnyǔ	phrase	phr.
主语	zhǔyǔ	subject	S
谓语	wèiyǔ	predicate	P
宾语	bīnyǔ	object	O
定语	dìngyǔ	attributive	Attrib
状语	zhuàngyǔ	adverbial	Adverb
补语	bǔyǔ	complement	C

CONTENTS

目录

1 Rènshi wǎngluò shèbèi
认识网络设备
Learning about Network Devices

Cháng yòng de wǎngluò shèbèi bāokuò diànnǎo、jiāohuànjī、 lùyóuqì、 fúwùqì děng,
常 用 的 网络 设备 包括 电脑、交换机、路由器、服务器 等，

kànkan tāmen zhījiān shì rúhé liánjiē qǐlái gōngzuò de.
看看 它们 之间 是 如何 连接 起来 工作 的。

Common network devices include the computer, switch, router, server, etc.

Let's take a look at how they connect and work together.

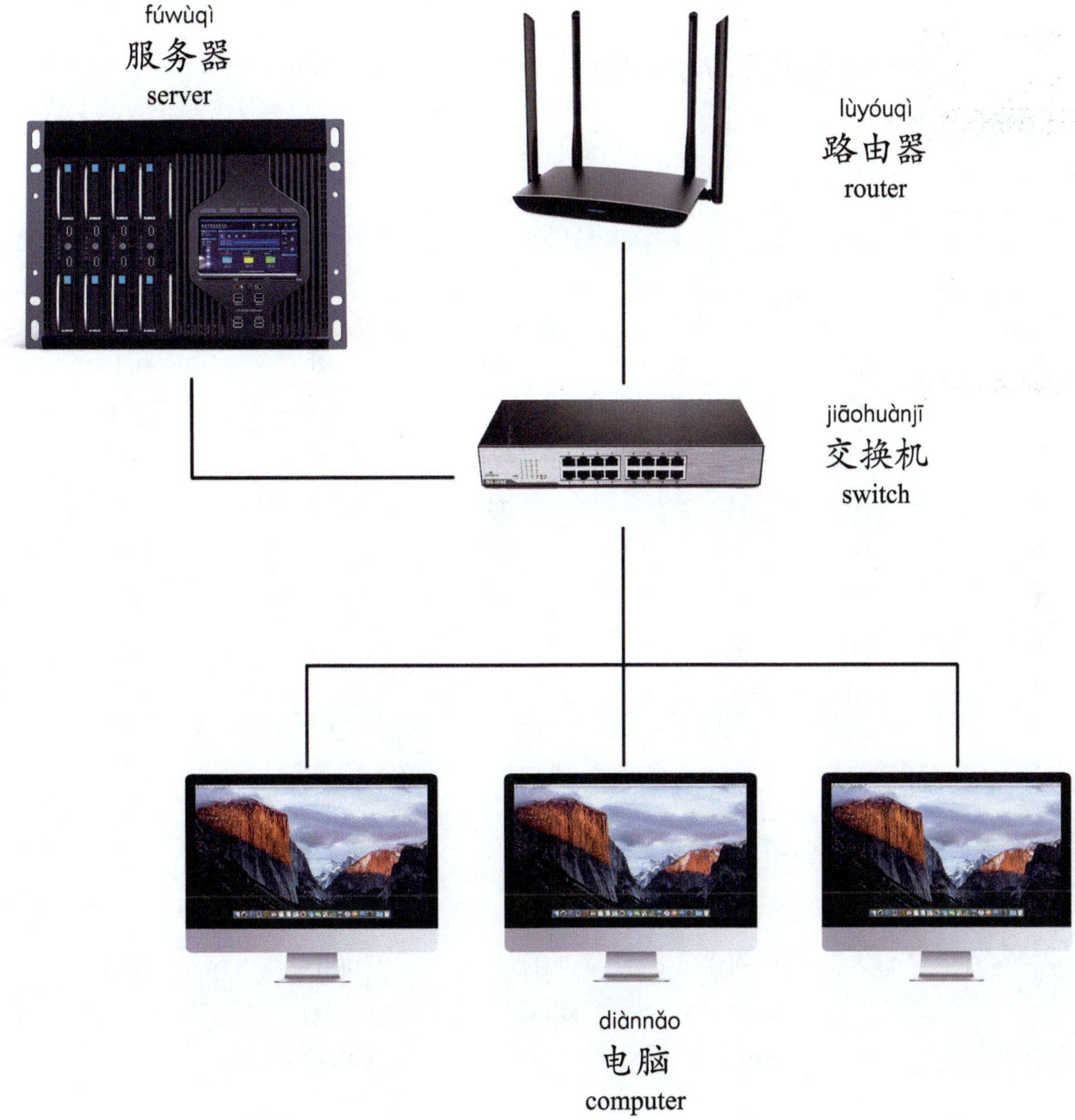

题解 Introduction

1. 学习内容：网络设备的基本功能及其在网络中的作用。
   Learning content: The basic functions of network devices and the role each device plays in the network.
2. 知识目标：学习声母、韵母和声调概貌，学习与网络设备相关的核心词语及表达。
   Knowledge target: Learn the basic knowledge of initials, finals and tones; master the key words and expressions related to network devices.
3. 技能目标：不同场景下，能准确判断和选择使用什么类型的交换机、网卡和路由器。
   Skill target: Be able to accurately judge and choose the proper types of switches, network interface cards (NICs) and routers according to different scenarios.

第一部分 Part 1

语音 Phonetic Learning

一、语音知识 yǔyīn zhīshi Knowledge about Phonetics

1. 声母和韵母（1） **Initials and finals (1)**

（1）声母表 Table of initials

声母 Initials	国际音标 International Phonetic Alphabet	声母 Initials	国际音标 International Phonetic Alphabet	声母 Initials	国际音标 International Phonetic Alphabet
b	[p]	g	[k]	zh	[tʂ]
p	[pʰ]	k	[kʰ]	ch	[tʂʰ]
m	[m]	h	[x]	sh	[ʂ]
f	[f]	j	[tɕ]	r	[ʐ]
d	[t]	q	[tɕʰ]	z	[ts]
t	[tʰ]	x	[ɕ]	c	[tsʰ]
n	[n]			s	[s]
l	[l]				

（2）韵母表 Table of finals

韵母 Finals	开口呼韵母 Open-mouth finals	齐齿呼韵母 Even-teeth finals	合口呼韵母 Closed-mouth finals	撮口呼韵母 Round-mouth finals
单韵母 Single Finals	-i[ɿ]、-i[ʅ]	i[i]	u[u]	ü[y]
	ɑ[A]	iɑ[iA]	uɑ[uA]	
	o[o]		uo[uo]	

（续表）

韵母 Finals	开口呼韵母 Open-mouth finals	齐齿呼韵母 Even-teeth finals	合口呼韵母 Closed-mouth finals	撮口呼韵母 Round-mouth finals
单韵母 Single Finals	e[ɤ]			
	er[ər]	ie[iɛ]		üe[yɛ]
复韵母 Compound Finals	ai[ai]		uai[uai]	
	ei[ei]		uei[uei]	
	ao[ɑu]	iao[iɑu]		
	ou[ou]	iou[iou]		
鼻韵母 Finals with a Nasal Consonant or Consonants	an[an]	ian[iɛn]	uan[uan]	üan[yan]
	en[ən]	in[in]	uen[uən]	ün[yn]
	ang[ɑŋ]	iang[iɑŋ]	uang[uɑŋ]	
	eng[əŋ]	ing[iŋ]	ueng[uəŋ]	
			ong[uŋ]	iong[yŋ]

2. 声调图 Figure of the tones

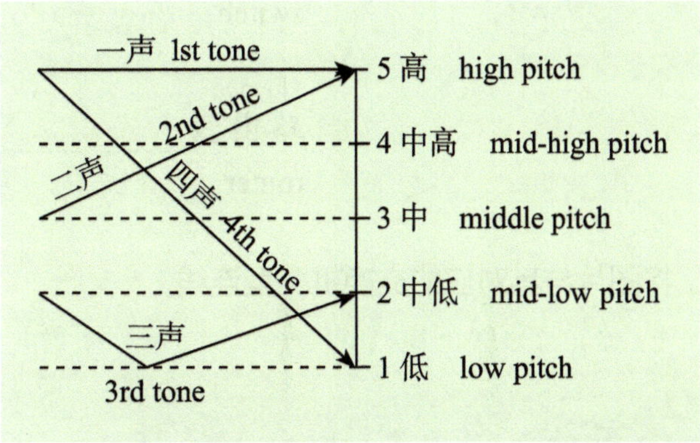

二、语音练习 yǔyīn liànxí Phonetic Exercises

1. 声韵调拼读 Spell and read.

b + ō = bō　　b + ó = bó　　b + ǒ = bǒ

b + ò = bò　　d + ī = dī　　d + í = dí

d + ǐ = dǐ　　d + ì = dì　　f + ā = fā

f + á = fá　　f + ǎ = fǎ　　f + à = fà

2. 读一读 Let's read.

① túdì 徒弟　② shīfu 师傅　③ bǐjìběn 笔记本　④ diànnǎo 电 脑

⑤ táishì 台式　⑥ zhǔjī 主机　⑦ xiǎnshìqì 显示器　⑧ jiànpán 键盘

⑨ shǔbiāo 鼠标　⑩ gāosù 高速　⑪ biànjié 便捷　⑫ wěndìng 稳定

第二部分　Part 2

课文 Texts

一、热身 rèshēn Warm-up

1. 给词语选择对应的图片。 **Match the pictures with corresponding words.**

A.

B.

C.

D.

① fúwùqì 服务器______ server　② jiāohuànjī 交换机______ switch

③ diànnǎo 电脑______ computer　④ lùyóuqì 路由器______ router

2. 观看介绍交换机的视频，将图片与其对应的交换机类型连线。

Watch the video about switches and match the pictures with the corresponding types of switches.

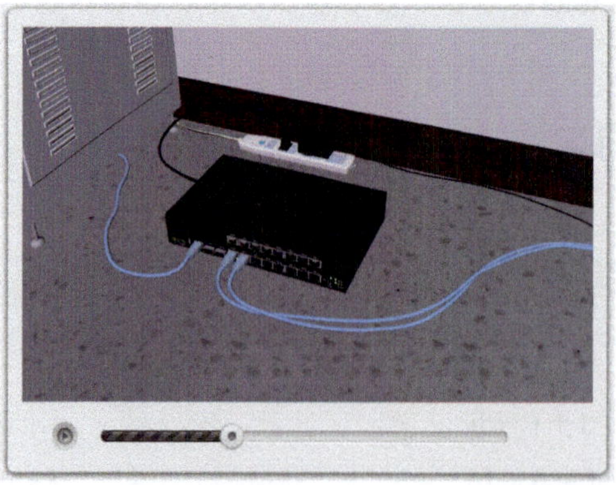

A. 
B. 
C. 
D. 

① èrshí sì kǒu 二十四口 24 ports　② sìshí bā kǒu 四十八口 48 ports　③ bā kǒu 八口 8 ports　④ shíliù kǒu 十六口 16 ports

二、课文 kèwén Texts

A 01-01

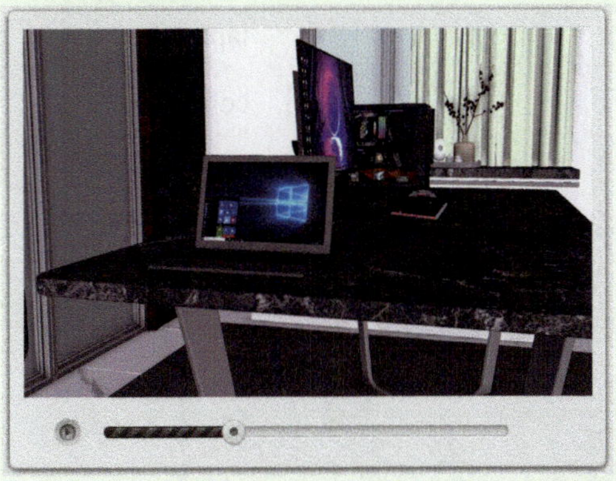

túdì: Shīfu, zhè shì shénme?
徒弟：师傅，这是什么？

shīfu: Zhè shì bǐjìběn diànnǎo.
师傅：这是笔记本电脑。

túdì: Nà shì shénme?
徒弟：那是什么？

shīfu: Nà shì táishì diànnǎo.
师傅：那是台式电脑。

译文 yìwén Text in English

Apprentice: Hello, Master! What's this?
Master: This is a laptop.
Apprentice: What's that?
Master: That's a desktop computer.

普通词语 pǔtōng cíyǔ General Vocabulary 01-02

1.	这	zhè	pron.	this
2.	是	shì	v.	be
3.	什么	shénme	pron.	what
4.	那	nà	pron.	that

专业词语 zhuānyè cíyǔ Specialized Vocabulary

01-03

1.	徒弟	túdì	n.	apprentice
2.	师傅	shīfu	n.	master
3.	笔记本	bǐjìběn	n.	laptop
4.	电脑	diànnǎo	n.	computer
5.	台式	táishì	adj.	desktop

B

01-04

túdì: Qǐngwèn diànnǎo yìbān yóu nǎxiē bùfen zǔchéng ne?
徒弟：请问　电脑一般由哪些部分组成呢？

shīfu: Diànnǎo yìbān yóu zhǔjī、 xiǎnshìqì、 jiànpán hé shǔbiāo děng zǔchéng.
师傅：电脑一般由主机、显示器、键盘和鼠标 等 组成。

译文 yìwén Text in English

Apprentice: What does a computer consist of?

Master: A computer usually consists of a host system unit, a monitor, a keyboard, a mouse, and so on.

普通词语 pǔtōng cíyǔ General Vocabulary

01-05

1.	请问	qǐngwèn	v.	excuse me, may I ask
2.	一般	yìbān	adv.	usually, generally

3.	由	yóu	prep.	by
4.	哪些	nǎxiē	pron.	which ones
5.	部分	bùfen	n.	part
6.	组成	zǔchéng	v.	consist of
7.	呢	ne	part.	*used at the end of an interrogative sentence*
8.	和	hé	conj.	and
9.	等	děng	part.	and so on, etc.

专业词语 zhuānyè cíyǔ Specialized Vocabulary

01-06

1.	主机	zhǔjī	n.	host
2.	显示器	xiǎnshìqì	n.	monitor
3.	键盘	jiànpán	n.	keyboard
4.	鼠标	shǔbiāo	n.	mouse

三、视听说 shì-tīng-shuō Viewing, Listening & Speaking

1. 观看介绍网卡的视频，将网卡与它们的特点连线。**Watch the video about network interface cards, and match the NICs with the corresponding characteristics.**

A. 高速 (gāosù) high-speed

B. 便捷 (biànjié) convenient

C. 稳定 (wěndìng) stable

① 服务器网卡 (fúwùqì wǎngkǎ) server NIC

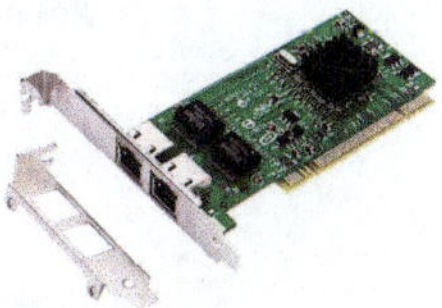

② 有线网卡 (yǒuxiàn wǎngkǎ) wired NIC

③ 无线网卡 (wúxiàn wǎngkǎ) wireless NIC

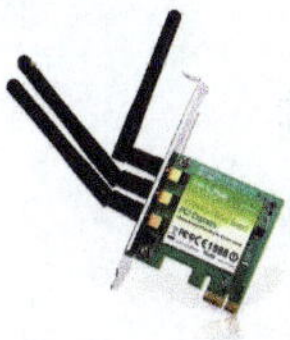

2. 说一说　**Let's talk.**

请说出各种网卡的名称和主要优势。

Please tell the names and main advantages of various NICs.

四、学以致用　xuéyǐzhìyòng　Practicing What You Have Learnt

观看介绍路由器类型的视频，判断各个地方应该选择使用什么类型的路由器，并将它们连线。

Watch the video about the router types, judge which types of routers should be used in places, and match the places with the corresponding routers.

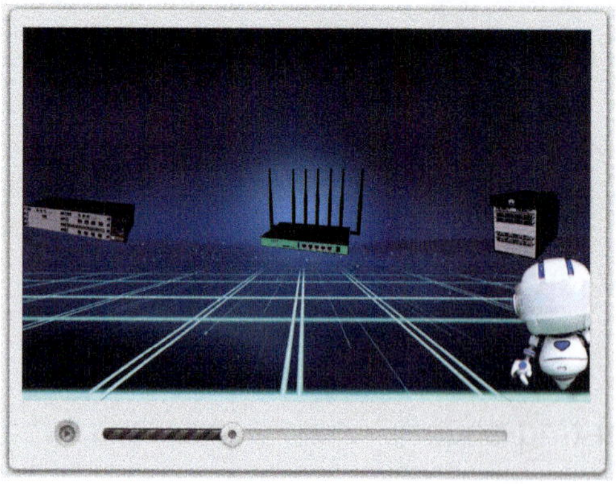

A.

B.

C.

D.

E.

① gǔgànjí lùyóuqì 骨干级路由器 backbone router

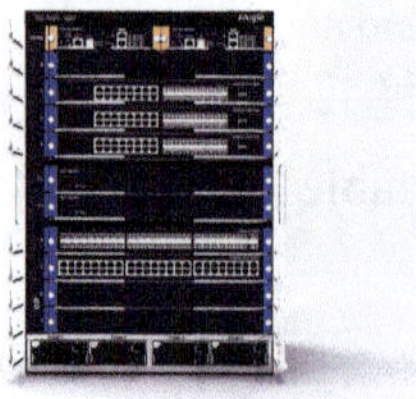

② qǐyèjí lùyóuqì 企业级路由器 enterprise-router

③ jiērùjí lùyóuqì 接入级路由器 access-router

补充专业词语　bǔchōng zhuānyè cíyǔ　Supplementary Specialized Vocabulary　01-07

1.	高速	gāosù	adj.	high-speed
2.	便捷	biànjié	adj.	convenient
3.	稳定	wěndìng	adj.	stable

4.	服务器网卡	fúwùqì wǎngkǎ	phr.	server NIC
5.	有线网卡	yǒuxiàn wǎngkǎ	phr.	wired NIC
6.	无线网卡	wúxiàn wǎngkǎ	phr.	wireless NIC
7.	骨干级路由器	gǔgànjí lùyóuqì	phr.	backbone router
8.	企业级路由器	qǐyèjí lùyóuqì	phr.	enterprise router
9.	接入级路由器	jiērùjí lùyóuqì	phr.	access router

第三部分 Part 3

课堂用语 Classroom Expressions

1. 你好。Nǐ hǎo. Hello.
2. 现在上课。Xiànzài shàngkè. Class begins.
3. 现在下课。Xiànzài xiàkè. Class is over.

第四部分 Part 4

单元实训 Unit Practical Training

认识网络设备 rènshi wǎngluò shèbèi Learning about Network Devices

实训目的 Training purpose

认识常用的网络设备，了解它们的工作过程，培养团队合作精神、竞争意识。

Learn about common network devices and their working process, and cultivate the spirit of teamwork and awareness of competition.

实训组织 Training organization

每组 3 ~ 5 人，选出一个组长。

Students work in groups of 3-5. Each group chooses a group leader.

实训内容 Training content

认识常用网络设备。

Getting to know common network devices.

实训步骤 Training steps

❶ 在计算机机房认识本单元学习的网络设备——电脑的基本组成部分、交换机、路由器、网卡、服务器，并了解它们的工作过程。

Recognize the network devices learnt in this unit in the computer room: basic components of the computer, switch, router, NIC, server, and learn about their working process.

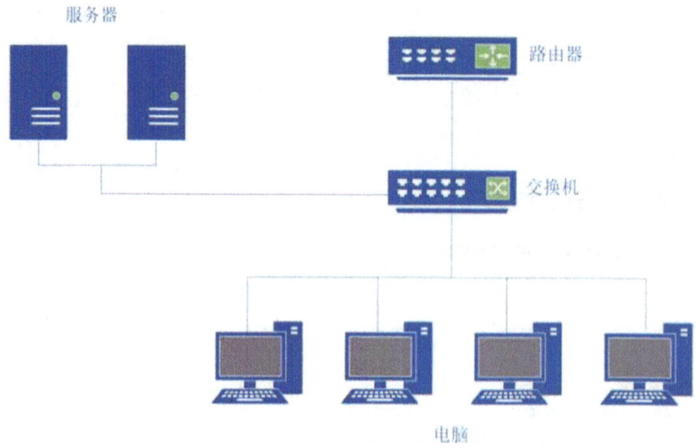

❷ 将参加实训的人员分成若干小组，每组 3 ～ 5 人。

Divide the students into groups of 3-5.

❸ 宣布比赛规则及要求：比赛题目分为必答题与抢答题两部分，每部分各 5 题，每题 10 分，共 100 分。小组成员需在 15 秒内说出图片上设备的名字，每题答对，得 10 分，答错或不答得 0 分。

Announce the rules and requirements of the competition: The competition consists of 5 required questions and 5 rapid-fire questions with 10 points for each question, totaling 100 points. For each question, the group members are required to speak out the name of the device in the picture within 15 seconds. For a correct answer, the group will get 10 points, while for a wrong answer or no answer, the group will get 0 point.

❹ 开始比赛。

The competition begins.

❺ 计算每组得分。

Calculate the scores for each group.

❻ 学员总结，教师总评。

The students make a summary and the teacher comments on the training.

第五部分 Part 5

单元小结 Unit Summary

cíyǔ
词语
Vocabulary

普通词语 General Vocabulary

1.	这	zhè	pron.	this
2.	是	shì	v.	be
3.	什么	shénme	pron.	what
4.	那	nà	pron.	that
5.	请问	qǐngwèn	v.	excuse me, may I ask
6.	一般	yìbān	adv.	usually, generally
7.	由	yóu	prep.	by
8.	哪些	nǎxiē	pron.	which ones
9.	部分	bùfen	n.	part
10.	组成	zǔchéng	v.	consist of
11.	呢	ne	part.	*used at the end of an interrogative sentence*
12.	和	hé	conj.	and
13.	等	děng	part.	and so on, etc.

专业词语 Specialized Vocabulary

1.	徒弟	túdì	n.	apprentice
2.	师傅	shīfu	n.	master
3.	笔记本	bǐjìběn	n.	laptop
4.	电脑	diànnǎo	n.	computer
5.	台式	táishì	adj.	desktop
6.	主机	zhǔjī	n.	host
7.	显示器	xiǎnshìqì	n.	monitor
8.	键盘	jiànpán	n.	keyboard
9.	鼠标	shǔbiāo	n.	mouse

补充专业词语 Supplementary Specialized Vocabulary

1.	高速	gāosù	adj.	high-speed
2.	便捷	biànjié	adj.	convenient
3.	稳定	wěndìng	adj.	stable
4.	服务器网卡	fúwùqì wǎngkǎ	phr.	server NIC
5.	有线网卡	yǒuxiàn wǎngkǎ	phr.	wired NIC

cíyǔ 词语 Vocabulary	6.	无线网卡	wúxiàn wǎngkǎ	phr.	wireless NIC
	7.	骨干级路由器	gǔgànjí lùyóuqì	phr.	backbone router
	8.	企业级路由器	qǐyèjí lùyóuqì	phr.	enterprise router
	9.	接入级路由器	jiērùjí lùyóuqì	phr.	access router

jùzi
句子
Sentences

1. 这 / 那是什么？
2. 电脑有笔记本电脑和台式电脑。
3. 电脑一般由主机、显示器、键盘和鼠标等组成。
4. 网卡一般有有线网卡、无线网卡、服务器网卡等类型。
5. 路由器从功能上可以划分为骨干级、企业级和接入级三种类型。

2

Shǐyòng wǎngxiàn

使用网线

Using the Network Cable

zhìzuò yì gēn zhítōngxiàn de bùzhòu

制作一根 直通线的步骤

Steps of Making a Straight-through Cable

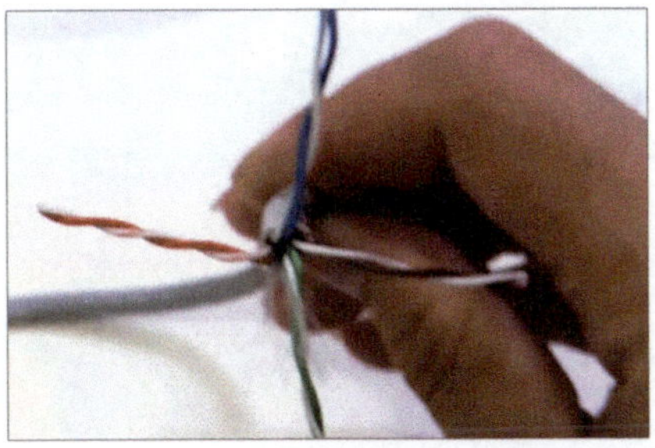

bāo xiàn
剥 线
strip the cable

pái xiàn
排 线
arrange the cable

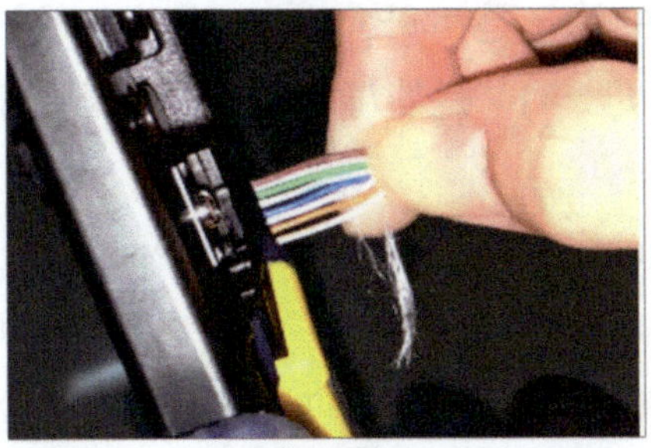

jiǎn xiàn
剪 线
cut the cable

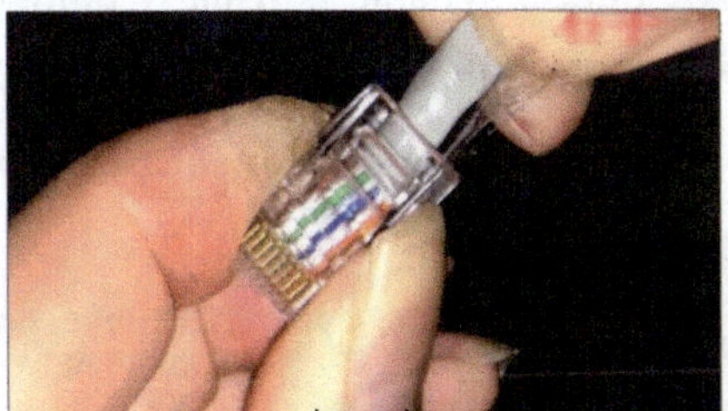

chā xiàn
插 线
insert the cable

yā xiàn
压 线
crimp the cable

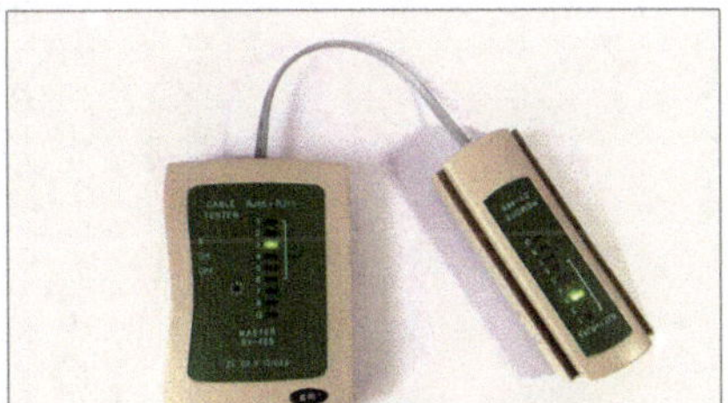

cè xiàn
测 线
test the cable

题解 Introduction

1. 学习内容：网线的主要分类和它们的作用。
   Learning content: The main types and functions of network cables
2. 知识目标：了解音节、声调的基本知识，掌握 b、p、m、f、d、t、n、l、g、k、h 等声母及开口呼韵母的发音，掌握与网线相关的核心词语及表达。
   Knowledge target: Learn about the basic knowledge of syllables and tones; master the pronunciation of the initials b, p, m, f, d, t, n, l, g, k, h and the open-mouth finals; master the key words and expressions related to network cables.
3. 技能目标：能制作一根交叉线和一根直通线。
   Skill target: Be able to make a crossover cable and a straight-through cable.

第一部分 Part 1

语音 Phonetic Learning

一、语音知识 yǔyīn zhīshi Knowledge about Phonetics

1. 音节 Syllables

汉语的音节一般由声母、韵母和声调组成，音节开头的辅音是声母，声母后面的部分是韵母，韵母上面的部分是声调。例如，在音节“nǐ”中，“n”是声母，“i”是韵母，“ˇ”是声调。音节也可以没有声母，只有韵母和声调，例如“é”。

A Chinese syllable is usually composed of an initial, a final and a tone. The consonant that starts a syllable is called the initial, and the part after the initial is the final. For example, in “nǐ”, “n” is the initial, “i” is the final, and “ˇ” is the tone mark. Some syllables do not have initials. A final and a tone can also make a syllable, such as “é”.

声母 Initials	韵母 Finals	声调 Tones	音节 Syllables
n	i	ˇ	nǐ
b	a	ˉ	bā
d	ian	ˋ	diàn
h	ao	ˇ	hǎo
	e	ˊ	é

2. 声母和韵母（2） Initials and finals (2)

（1）声母 Initials：b p m f d t n l g k h

声母 Initials	国际音标 International Phonetic Alphabet	声母 Initials	国际音标 International Phonetic Alphabet	声母 Initials	国际音标 International Phonetic Alphabet
b	[p]	d	[t]	g	[k]
p	[pʰ]	t	[tʰ]	k	[kʰ]
m	[m]	n	[n]	h	[x]
f	[f]	l	[l]		

（2）开口呼韵母 Open-mouth finals

开口呼韵母 Open-mouth finals	国际音标 International Phonetic Alphabet	开口呼韵母 Open-mouth finals	国际音标 International Phonetic Alphabet	开口呼韵母 Open-mouth finals	国际音标 International Phonetic Alphabet
-i	[ɿ]	ai	[ai]	an	[an]
-i	[ʅ]	ei	[ei]	en	[ən]
a	[A]	ao	[ɑu]	ang	[ɑŋ]
o	[o]	ou	[ou]	eng	[əŋ]
e	[ɤ]				
er	[ər]				

3. 声调 Tones

汉语是有声调的语言，声调不同，意义就可能不一样。

汉语普通话有四个基本声调。标识声调的符号有四个："ˉ" 表示第一声，"ˊ" 表示第二声，"ˇ" 表示第三声，"ˋ" 表示第四声。调号标在主要元音的上边，如 mā、má、mǎ、mà。

Chinese is a tonal language. Different tones may result in different meanings.

There are four basic tones in Mandarin Chinese. They are marked as "ˉ" (the 1st tone), "ˊ" (the 2nd tone), "ˇ" (the 3rd tone) and "ˋ" (the 4th tone) respectively. Tones are marked above the main vowel. For example, "mā", "má", "mǎ", "mà".

二、语音练习 yǔyīn liànxí Phonetic Exercises

读一读 Let's read.

① shuǐjīngtóu 水晶头
② jiētóu 接头
③ cèxiànyí 测线仪
④ wǎngluò 网络
⑤ liántōngxìng 连通性
⑥ bāoxiànqián 剥线钳
⑦ shuāngjiǎoxiàn 双绞线
⑧ chuánshū jièzhì 传输 介质
⑨ zhítōngxiàn 直通线
⑩ jiāochāxiàn 交叉线
⑪ jiǎowèi 脚位
⑫ zhèxiē 这些

第二部分 Part 2

课文 Texts

一、热身 rèshēn Warm-up

1. 给下列设备和工具选择对应的图片。

Choose the corresponding pictures for the following devices and tools.

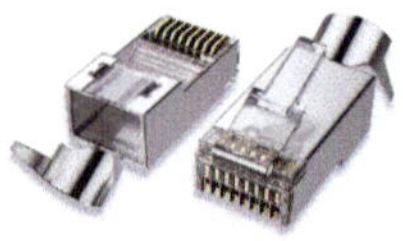

A.

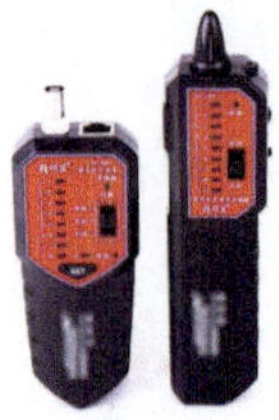

B.

C.

D.

① shuāngjiǎoxiàn 双绞线 ________________ twisted pair

② bāoxiànqián 剥线钳 ________________ wire strippers

③ cèxiànyí 测线仪________________ cable tester

④ RJ45 shuǐjīngtóu RJ45 水晶头 ________________ RJ45 plug

2. 观看介绍各种设备、工具的视频，将它们与各自的用途连线。

Watch the video about various tools and devices, and match them with their corresponding uses.

chuánshū
A. 传 输
transmit

cèshì
B. 测试
test

bāochú
C. 剥除
strip

liánjiē
D. 连接
connect

RJ45 shuǐjīngtóu
① RJ45 水晶头
RJ45 plug

cèxiànyí
② 测线仪
cable tester

shuāngjiǎoxiàn
③ 双 绞 线
twisted pair

bāoxiànqián
④ 剥线钳
wire strippers

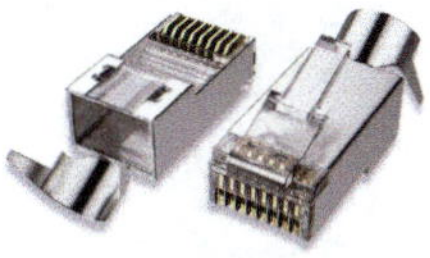
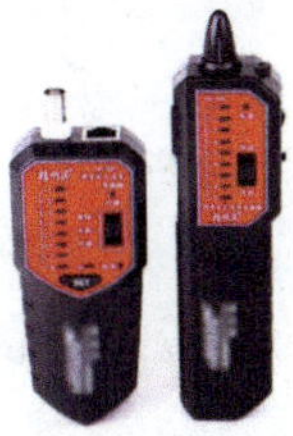

二、课文 kèwén Texts

A 02-01

túdì: Shīfu, qǐngwèn zhèxiē shì shénme?
徒弟：师傅，请问 这些是什么？

shīfu: Zhèxiē shì RJ45 shuǐjīngtóu.
师傅：这些是 RJ45 水晶头。

túdì: Shuǐjīngtóu shì yònglái zuò shénme de?
徒弟：水晶头 是用来做 什么的？

shīfu: Shuǐjīngtóu shì wǎngluò liánjiē zhōng zhòngyào de jiētóu.
师傅：水晶头 是 网络 连接 中 重要 的接头。

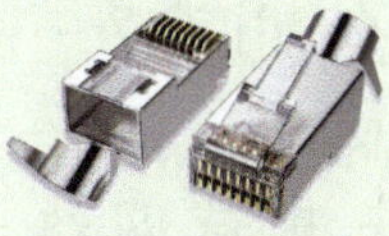

译文 yìwén Text in English

Apprentice: Master, what are these?
Master: These are RJ45 plugs.
Apprentice: What is the plug used for?
Master: The plug is an important connector in the network connection.

普通词语 pǔtōng cíyǔ General Vocabulary

02-02

1.	这些	zhèxiē	pron.	these
2.	用来	yònglái	phr.	be used to/for
3.	做	zuò	v.	do, make
4.	是……的	shì···de	phr.	*a phrase used to categorize sth.*
	的	de	part.	*a modal particle used at the end of a sentence to indicate an affirmative tone*
5.	连接	liánjiē	v.	connect
6.	中	zhōng	n.	middle, center
7.	重要	zhòngyào	adj.	important

专业词语 zhuānyè cíyǔ Specialized Vocabulary

02-03

1.	RJ45 水晶头	RJ45 shuǐjīngtóu	phr.	RJ45 plug
2.	接头	jiētóu	n.	connector

B 02-04

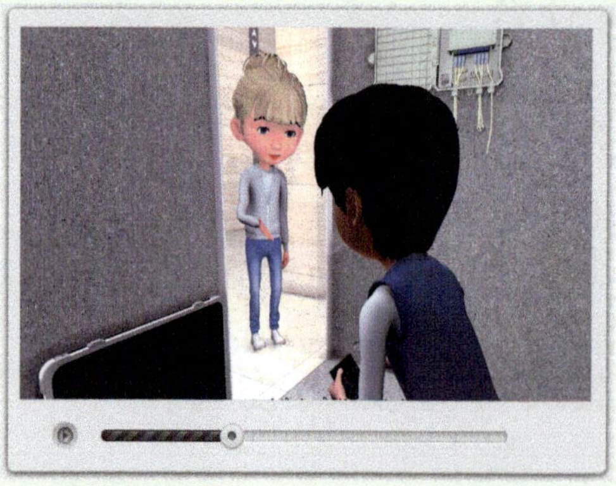

túdì: Cèxiànyí yǒu shénme yòngtú?
徒弟：测线仪有什么用途？

shīfu: Cèxiànyí shì yònglái cèshì wǎngluò liántōngxìng de.
师傅：测线仪是用来测试网络连通性的。

túdì: Nà bāoxiànqián ne?
徒弟：那剥线钳呢？

shīfu: Bāoxiànqián shì yònglái bāochú shuāngjiǎoxiàn wài pí de.
师傅：剥线钳是用来剥除双绞线外皮的。

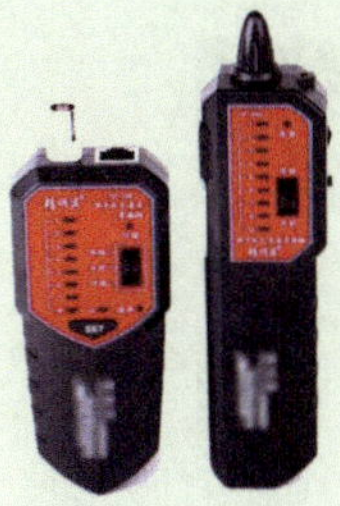

译文 yìwén Text in English

Apprentice: What is the cable tester used for?
Master: It is used to test the network's connectivity.
Apprentice: How about the wire strippers?
Master: They are used to strip the twisted pair's sheath.

普通词语 pǔtōng cíyǔ General Vocabulary

02-05

1.	有	yǒu	v.	have
2.	用途	yòngtú	n.	use, application
3.	测试	cèshì	v.	test
4.	那	nà	conj.	so, and
5.	剥除	bāochú	phr.	strip
6.	外皮	wài pí	phr.	outer sheath

专业词语 zhuānyè cíyǔ Specialized Vocabulary

02-06

1.	测线仪	cèxiànyí	n.	cable tester
2.	网络	wǎngluò	n.	network
3.	连通性	liántōngxìng	n.	connectivity
4.	剥线钳	bāoxiànqián	n.	wire strippers
5.	双绞线	shuāngjiǎoxiàn	n.	twisted pair

三、视听说 shì-tīng-shuō Viewing, Listening & Speaking

1. 观看介绍网线制作的视频，并将网线与它们各自的作用进行连线。

Watch the video about the process of making network cables, and match the cables with their corresponding functions.

zhítōngxiàn
① 直通线
straight-through cable

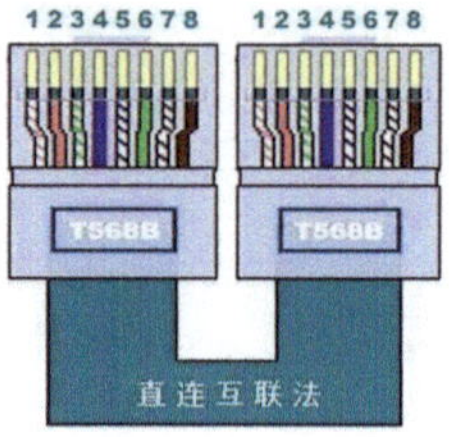

liánjiē yì zhǒng shèbèi
A. 连接异 种 设备
connecting different kinds of devices

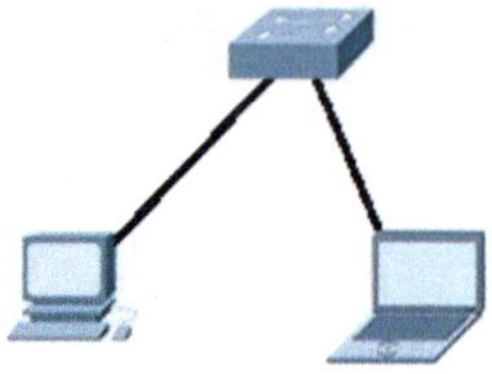

jiāochāxiàn
② 交叉线
crossover cable

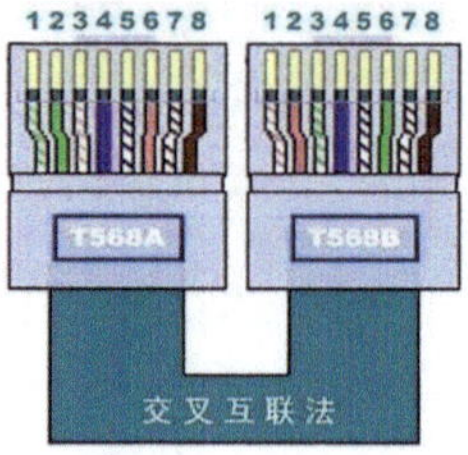

liánjiē tóng zhǒng shèbèi
B. 连接同 种 设备
connecting the same kind of devices

2. 说一说 **Let's talk.**

请复述视频中的关键词，并说出网线的分类。

Please repeat the key words in the video, and speak out the classification of network cables.

四、学以致用 xuéyǐzhìyòng Practicing What You Have Learnt

观看介绍如何制作一根直通线的视频，并按 T568B 标准填写线序。

Watch the video about the process of making a straight-through cable, and put the wires in correct order according to standard T568B.

chéngsè A. 橙色	lánsè B. 蓝色	lǜ-báisè C. 绿白色	chéng-báisè D. 橙白色
zōngsè E. 棕色	lán-báisè F. 蓝白色	zōng-báisè G. 棕白色	lǜsè H. 绿色

jiǎowèi 脚位 Pin	1	2	3	4	5	6	7	8
T568B	____	____	____	____	____	____	____	____

补充专业词语 bǔchōng zhuānyè cíyǔ Supplementary Specialized Vocabulary

02-07

1.	传输介质	chuánshū jièzhì	phr.	transmission medium
2.	直通线	zhítōngxiàn	n.	straight-through cable
3.	交叉线	jiāochāxiàn	n.	crossover cable
4.	脚位	jiǎowèi	n.	Pin no

第三部分 Part 3

课堂用语 Classroom Expressions

1. 跟我读。Gēn wǒ dú. Read after me.
2. 读课文。Dú kèwén. Read the text.

第四部分 Part 4

单元实训 Unit Practical Training

制作一根交叉线 zhìzuò yì gēn jiāochāxiàn Making a Crossover Cable

实训目的 Training purpose

认识本单元学习的网络设备，学会制作一根交叉线。

Learn about the network devices in this unit, and learn to make a crossover cable.

实训组织 Training organization

每组 3 ～ 5 人。选出一个组长。

Students work in groups of 3-5. Each group chooses a group leader.

实训内容 Training content

制作一根交叉线。

Making a crossover cable.

实训步骤 Training steps

1. 剥线。用剥线钳划开其外保护套，刀口距五类双绞线至少 2 厘米。

   Strip the cable: Cut the outer protective sheath of the cable with the wire strippers and the cut should be at least 2cm away from the CAT-5 twisted pair.

2. 排线。交叉线的线芯一端按照 T568B 标准进行导线颜色排线，另一端则按照 T568A 标准进行导线颜色排线。

   Arrange the wires: One ends of the wires should be arranged by their colors in accordance with standard T568B, and the other ends are arranged by their colors in accordance with standard T568A.

3. 剪线。用压线钳剪断 8 根导线（剪平）。

   Cut the wires: Cut 8 wires with the crimping pliers (flat cut).

4. 插线。一只手捏住水晶头，将有弹片的一侧向下，有针脚的一端指向远离自己的方向；另一只手捏平双绞线，最左边是第一脚，最右边是第八脚。

   Insert the cable: Hold the plug with one hand, making the end with a clip pointing downward and the end with pins away from yourself; pinch the twisted pair with the other hand flat, making the leftmost being the first pin and the rightmost being the eighth pin.

⑤ 压线。在确认一切无误后，将 RJ45 水晶头放入压线钳的压头槽内压实。

Crimp the cable: After confirming that everything has been done correctly, put the RJ45 plug into the slot of the crimping pliers and crimp it tightly.

⑥ 测线。测线仪主机灯从 1 至 8 依次闪烁，副机这边灯亮的顺序为：3、6、1、4、5、2、7、8，表明交叉线制作成功。

Test the cable: The indicator lights of the cable tester's mainframe flash successively from 1 to 8, and the lights of the auxiliary machine flash in the sequence of 3, 6, 1, 4, 5, 2, 7, 8, indicating that the crossover cable has been successfully made.

⑦ 学员总结，教师总评。

The trainees make a summary and the teacher comments on the training.

第五部分 Part 5

单元小结 Unit Summary

cíyǔ
词语
Vocabulary

普通词语 General Vocabulary

1.	这些	zhèxiē	pron.	these
2.	用来	yònglái	phr.	be used to/for
3.	做	zuò	v.	do, make
4.	是……的	shì…de	phr.	*a phrase used to categorize sth.*
	的	de	part.	*a modal particle used at the end of a sentence to indicate an affirmative tone*
5.	连接	liánjiē	v.	connect
6.	中	zhōng	n.	middle, center
7.	重要	zhòngyào	adj.	important
8.	有	yǒu	v.	have
9.	用途	yòngtú	n.	use, application
10.	测试	cèshì	v.	test
11.	那	nà	conj.	so, and
12.	剥除	bāochú	phr.	strip
13.	外皮	wài pí	phr.	outer sheath

专业词语 Specialized Vocabulary

1.	RJ45 水晶头	RJ45 shuǐjīngtóu	phr.	RJ45 plug
2.	接头	jiētóu	n.	connector
3.	测线仪	cèxiànyí	n.	cable tester
4.	网络	wǎngluò	n.	network

cíyǔ
词语
Vocabulary

5.	连通性	liántōngxìng	n.	connectivity
6.	剥线钳	bāoxiànqián	n.	wire strippers
7.	双绞线	shuāngjiǎoxiàn	n.	twisted pair

补充专业词语　Supplementary Specialized Vocabulary

1.	传输介质	chuánshū jièzhì	phr.	transmission medium
2.	直通线	zhítōngxiàn	n.	straight-through cable
3.	交叉线	jiāochāxiàn	n.	crossover cable
4.	脚位	jiǎowèi	n.	Pin no

jùzi
句子
Sentences

1. 这些 / 那些是什么？
2. 测线仪是用来测试网络连通性的。
3. 网线一般分为直通线和交叉线。
4. 直通线用于异种设备的连接。
5. 交叉线用于同种设备的连接。

3

Shǐyòng guāngxiān

使用光纤

Using the Optical Fiber

guāngxiān tiàoxiàn de chājiē

光纤 跳线的插接

Insertion of the Fiber-Optic Patch Cord

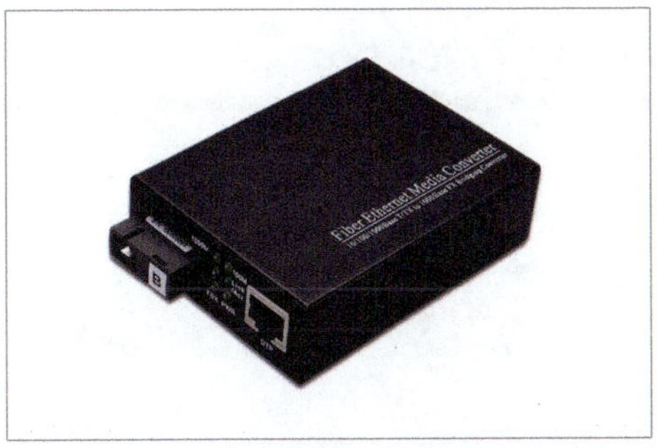

jiāng yí gè guāngxiān mókuài chārù wǎngluò shèbèi

将一个 光纤 模块 插入网络 设备

insert a fiber-optic module into the network device

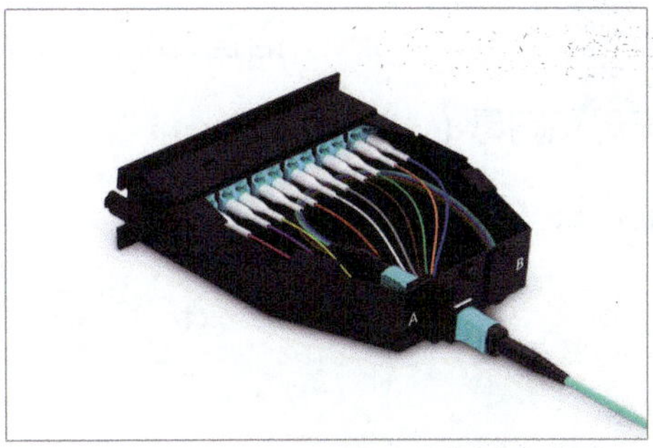

xuǎnzé héshì de guāngxiān tiàoxiàn bìng

选择合适的 光纤 跳线 并

chārù guāngxiān mókuài

插入 光纤 模块

choose the appropriate fiber-optic patch cord

and insert it into the fiber-optic module

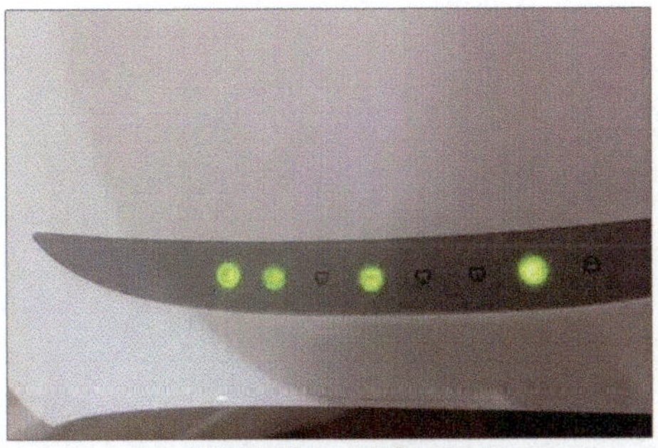

zhǐshìdēng shǎnshuò

指示灯 闪烁

the indicator light flashes

wánchéng tiàoxiàn de chājiē

完成 跳线的插接

complete the insertion of the patch cord

题解　Introduction

1. 学习内容：光纤的使用，单模光纤和多模光纤的区别和特点。
   Learning content: The use of the optical fiber; the differences between and characteristics of the single-mode and multi-mode optical fibers.
2. 知识目标：了解轻声的基本知识，掌握 zh、ch、sh、r、z、c、s 等声母及合口呼韵母的发音，掌握与光纤相关的核心词语及表达。
   Knowledge target: Learn about the basic knowledge of the neutral tone; master the pronunciation of the initials zh, ch, sh, r, z, c, s and the closed-mouth finals; master the key words and expressions related to the optical fiber.
3. 技能目标：掌握光纤跳线的插接。
   Skill target: Master the process of inserting the fiber-optic patch cord.

第一部分　Part 1

语音　Phonetic Learning

一、语音知识　yǔyīn zhīshi　Knowledge about Phonetics

1. 声母和韵母（3）　Initials and finals (3)

（1）声母 Initials：zh ch sh r z c s

声母 Initials	国际音标 International Phonetic Alphabet	声母 Initials	国际音标 International Phonetic Alphabet
zh	[tʂ]	z	[ts]
ch	[tʂʰ]	c	[tsʰ]
sh	[ʂ]	s	[s]
r	[ʐ]		

（2）合口呼韵母 Closed–mouth finals

合口呼韵母 Closed-mouth finals	国际音标 International Phonetic Alphabet	合口呼韵母 Closed-mouth finals	国际音标 International Phonetic Alphabet	合口呼韵母 Closed-mouth finals	国际音标 International Phonetic Alphabet
u	[u]	uai	[uai]	uang	[uaŋ]
ua	[uA]	uei	[uei]	ueng	[uəŋ]
uo	[uo]	uan	[uan]	ong	[uŋ]
		uen	[uən]		

2. 轻声 Neutral tone

汉语里有些音节不带声调，念得又短又轻，拼写时不标号，这种念得又短又轻的声调叫轻声。例如：爸爸（bàba，dad）、妈妈（māma，mom）。

The neutral tone is pronounced lightly and briefly without any stress, and is indicated in Pinyin by the absence of any tone mark above the syllable. For example, “爸爸”(bàba, dad), “妈妈”(māma, mom).

二、语音练习 yǔyīn liànxí Phonetic Exercises

读一读 Let's read.

① dānmó guāngxiān 单模 光 纤	② duōmó guāngxiān 多模 光 纤	③ guāng 光	④ guāngxiānwǎng 光 纤 网
⑤ shèbèi 设备	⑥ tiào-jiē xiàn 跳接 线	⑦ guāngxiān tiàoxiàn 光 纤 跳线	⑧ guāngxiān mókuài 光 纤 模块
⑨ zhíjìng 直径	⑩ jùlí 距离	⑪ qūbié 区别	⑫ yánzhe 沿着

第二部分 Part 2

课文 Texts

一、热身 rèshēn Warm-up

1. 给词语选择对应的图片。 Match the pictures with corresponding words.

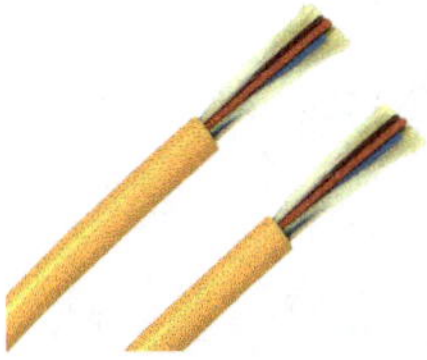

A.

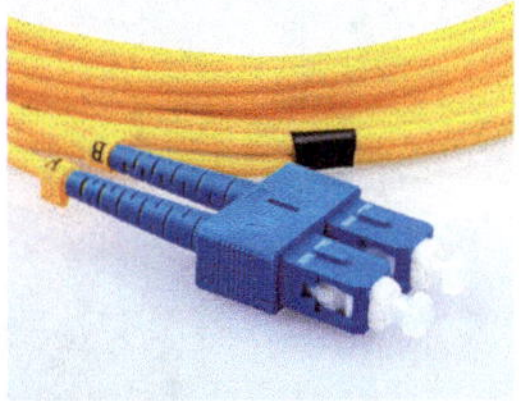

B.

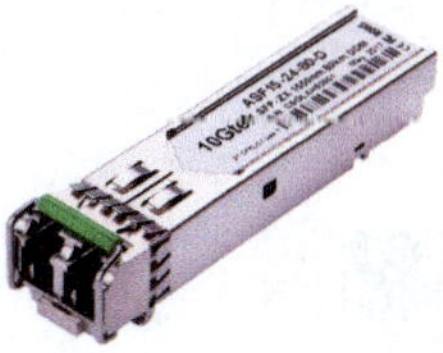

C.

D.

① dānmó guāngxiān 单模 光纤 ________________
single-mode optical fiber

② duōmó guāngxiān 多模 光纤 ________________
multi-mode optical fiber

③ guāngxiān mókuài 光纤 模块________________
fiber-optic module

④ guāngxiān tiàoxiàn 光纤 跳线________________
fiber-optic patch cord

2. 观看介绍光纤插接的视频，把相应的选项填写在横线上。

Watch the video about the insertion of the optical fiber, and choose corresponding answers to fill in the blanks.

guāngxiān mókuài
A. 光纤 模块
fiber-optic module

dānmó guāngxiān
B. 单模 光纤
single-mode optical fiber

guāngxiān tiàoxiàn
C. 光纤 跳线
fiber-optic patch cord

shèbèi
D. 设备
device

Shìpín zhōng shǐyòng de shì yì gēn
① 视频中使用的是一根______________。
There is a ______________ used in the video.

Guāngxiān tiàoxiàn chārù shèbèi de shùnxù shì
② 光纤跳线插入设备的顺序是______________。
The order that the fiber-optic patch cords are inserted in the device is ______________.

二、课文 kèwén Texts

A 03-01

túdì: Dānmó guāngxiān hé duōmó guāngxiān yǒu shénme qūbié?
徒弟：单模光纤和多模光纤有什么区别？

shīfu: Dānmó guāngxiān zhōng, guāng yánzhe yì tiáo lùjìng chuánbō; duōmó guāngxiān zhōng, guāng yánzhe duō tiáo lùjìng chuánbō.
师傅：单模光纤中，光沿着一条路径传播；多模光纤中，光沿着多条路径传播。

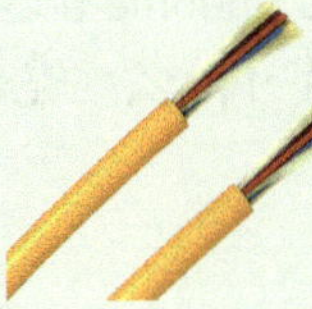

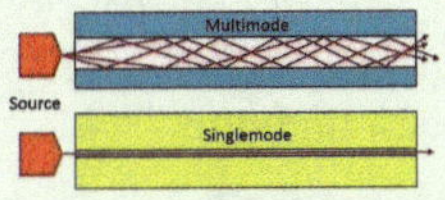

译文 yìwén Text in English

Apprentice: What is the difference between the single-mode optical fiber and the multi-mode optical fiber?

Master: In a single-mode optical fiber, the light travels along one path; while in a multi-mode optical fiber, the light travels along multiple paths.

普通词语 pǔtōng cíyǔ General Vocabulary

03-02

1.	区别	qūbié	n.	difference
2.	沿着	yánzhe	phr.	(be/go/travel) along
3.	一	yī	num.	one
4.	条	tiáo	m.	*used to indicate paths, trousers, etc.*
5.	路径	lùjìng	n.	path
6.	传播	chuánbō	v.	spread
7.	多	duō	adj.	many

专业词语 zhuānyè cíyǔ Specialized Vocabulary

03-03

1.	单模光纤	dānmó guāngxiān	phr.	single-mode optical fiber
	光纤	guāngxiān	n.	optical fiber
2.	多模光纤	duōmó guāngxiān	phr.	multi-mode optical fiber
3.	光	guāng	n.	light

B 03-04

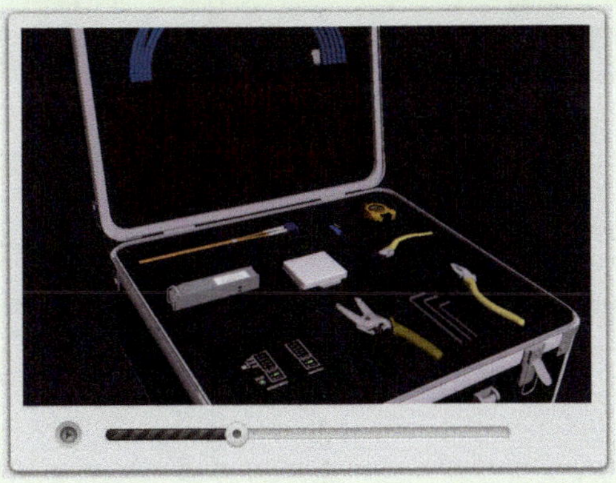

túdì: Shīfu, guāngxiānwǎng zhōng, cóng wǎngluò jiērù shèbèi xūyào shénme tiào-jiēxiàn?
徒弟：师傅，光纤网中，从网络接入设备需要什么跳接线？

shīfu: Guāngxiān tiàoxiàn.
师傅：光纤跳线。

túdì: Guāngxiān tiàoxiàn liánjiē shèbèi de shíhou yìbān xūyào shénme?
徒弟：光纤跳线连接设备的时候一般需要什么？

shīfu: Guāngxiān mókuài.
师傅：光纤模块。

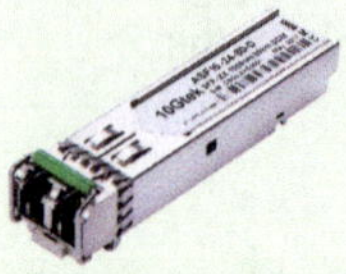

译文 yìwén Text in English

Apprentice: Master, in an optical fiber network, what kind of patch cord is needed to connect the device to the network?
Master: The fiber-optic patch cord.
Apprentice: What is needed when we connect the fiber-optic patch cord with the device?
Master: The fiber-optic module.

普通词语 pǔtōng cíyǔ General Vocabulary

03-05

1.	从	cóng	prep.	from
2.	接入	jiērù	phr.	connect...to...
3.	时候	shíhou	n.	time, moment
4.	需要	xūyào	aux.	need

专业词语 zhuānyè cíyǔ Specialized Vocabulary

03-06

1.	光纤网	guāngxiānwǎng	n.	optical fiber network
2.	设备	shèbèi	n.	equipment
3.	跳接线	tiào-jiēxiàn	n.	patch cord
4.	光纤跳线	guāngxiān tiàoxiàn	phr.	fiber-optic patch cord
5.	光纤模块	guāngxiān mókuài	phr.	fiber-optic module

三、视听说 shì-tīng-shuō Viewing, Listening & Speaking

1. 观看介绍光纤的视频，将单模光纤和多模光纤与各自的特点连线。

Watch the video about the optical fiber, and match the single-mode optical fiber and the multi-mode optical fiber with their characteristics.

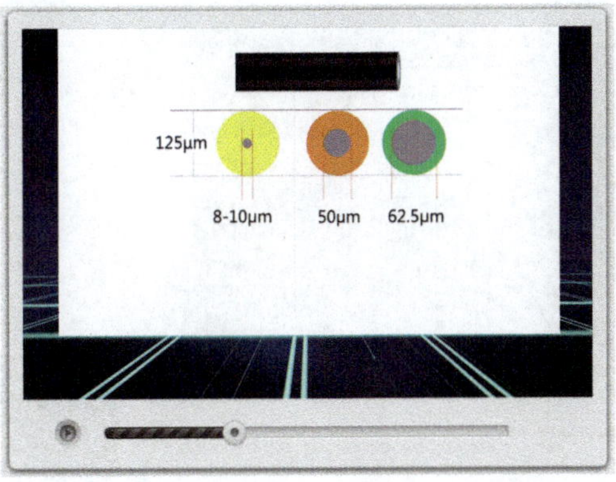

dānmó guāngxiān
① 单模 光纤
single-mode optical fiber

duōmó guāngxiān
② 多模 光纤
multi-mode optical fiber

zhíjìng jiào xiǎo
A. 直径 较 小
smaller diameter

zhíjìng jiào dà
B. 直径 较 大
bigger diameter

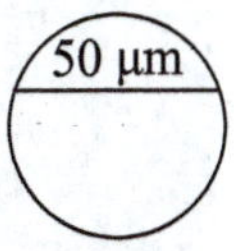

chuánshū jùlí jiào duǎn
C. 传输 距离 较 短
shorter transmission distance

chuánshū jùlí jiào cháng
D. 传输 距离 较 长
longer transmission distance

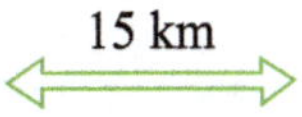

chéngsè hùtàopí
E. 橙色 护套皮
orange sheath

huángsè hùtàopí
F. 黄色 护套皮
yellow sheath

2. 说一说 **Let's talk.**

请模仿说出单模光纤和多模光纤的区别。

Please describe the differences between the single-mode optical fiber and the multi-mode optical fiber.

四、学以致用 xuéyǐzhìyòng Practicing What You Have Learnt

观看介绍不同光纤类型适用场景的视频，并根据视频为下列不同的光纤选择合适的场景。

Watch the video about the application scenarios that different types of optical fibers fit for, and choose appropriate scenarios for different optical fibers according to the video.

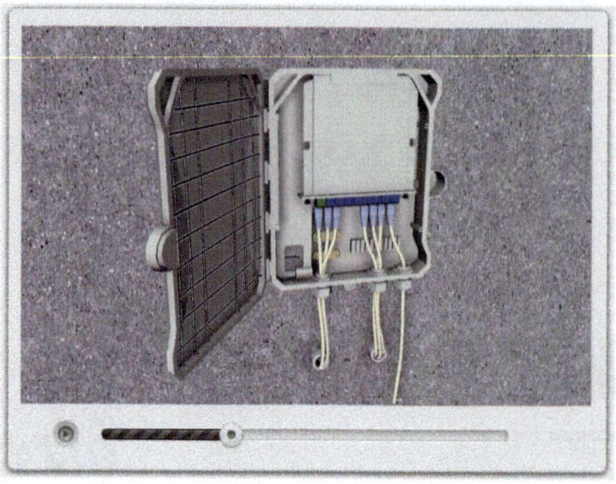

A.

B.

C.

D.

dānmó guāngxiān
① 单模 光纤 ____________
single-mode optical fiber

duōmó guāngxiān
② 多模 光纤 ____________
multi-mode optical fiber

补充专业词语 bǔchōng zhuānyè cíyǔ Supplementary Specialized Vocabulary

03-07

1.	直径	zhíjìng	n.	diameter
2.	距离	jùlí	n.	distance

第三部分 Part 3

课堂用语 Classroom Expressions

① 有问题吗？ Yǒu wèntí ma? Do you have any questions?

② 请再说一遍。Qǐng zài shuō yí biàn. Please say it again.

第四部分 Part 4

单元实训 *Unit Practical Training*

光纤跳线的插接 guāngxiān tiàoxiàn de chājiē Insertion of the Fiber-Optic Patch Cord

实训目的 Training purpose

了解光纤跳线如何接入光纤模块。

Learn about how to insert the fiber-optic patch cord into the fiber-optic module.

实训组织 Training organization

每组 3 ～ 5 人，选出一个组长。

Students work in groups of 3-5. Each group chooses a group leader.

实训内容 Training content

认识光纤设备，并学习跳线的插接。

Learning about fiber-optic equipment and learning how to insert the fiber-optic patch cord.

实训步骤 Training steps

1. 通过跟读、图片展示及小组知识问答比赛等方式认识光纤和本单元常用设备。
   Learn about the optical fiber and common equipment introduced in this unit through listening and repeating, picture presentation, group Q&A quiz and other methods.
2. 在交换机的光纤端口插入光纤模块；
   Insert the fiber-optic module into the fiber port of the switch;
3. 将光纤跳线两端插入光纤模块；
   Insert both ends of the fiber-optic patch cord into the fiber-optic module;
4. 观察指示灯是否闪烁；
   Note if the indicator light flashes;
5. 完成跳线的插接。
   Complete the insertion of the patch cord.
6. 学员总结，教师总评。
   The students make a summary and the teacher comments on the training.

第五部分 Part 5

单元小结 Unit Summary

cíyǔ
词语
Vocabulary

普通词语 General Vocabulary

1.	区别	qūbié	n.	difference
2.	沿着	yánzhe	phr.	(be/go/travel) along
3.	一	yī	num.	one
4.	条	tiáo	m.	*used to indicate paths, trousers, etc.*
5.	路径	lùjìng	n.	path
6.	传播	chuánbō	v.	spread
7.	多	duō	adj.	many
8.	从	cóng	prep.	from
9.	接入	jiērù	phr.	connect...to...
10.	时候	shíhou	n.	time, moment
11.	需要	xūyào	aux.	need

专业词语 Specialized Vocabulary

1.	单模光纤	dānmó guāngxiān	phr.	single-mode optical fiber
	光纤	guāngxiān	n.	optical fiber
2.	多模光纤	duōmó guāngxiān	phr.	multi-mode optical fiber
3.	光	guāng	n.	light
4.	光纤网	guāngxiānwǎng	n.	optical fiber network
5.	设备	shèbèi	n.	equipment
6.	跳接线	tiào-jiēxiàn	n.	patch cord
7.	光纤跳线	guāngxiān tiàoxiàn	phr.	fiber-optic patch cord
8.	光纤模块	guāngxiān mókuài	phr.	fiber-optic module

补充专业词语 Supplementary Specialized Vocabulary

1.	直径	zhíjìng	n.	diameter
2.	距离	jùlí	n.	distance

jùzi
句子
Sentences

1. 常用的光纤有单模光纤和多模光纤两种。
2. 单模光纤中，光沿着一条路径传播；多模光纤中，光沿着多条路径传播。
3. 光纤网中，从网络接入设备需要的跳接线是光纤跳线。
4. 光纤跳线连接设备的时候一般需要光纤模块。

4

Wǎngluò dìzhǐ

网络地址

Network Address

jìngtài IP dìzhǐ de shèzhì bùzhòu

静态 IP地址的 设置 步骤

Steps of Setting the Static IP Address

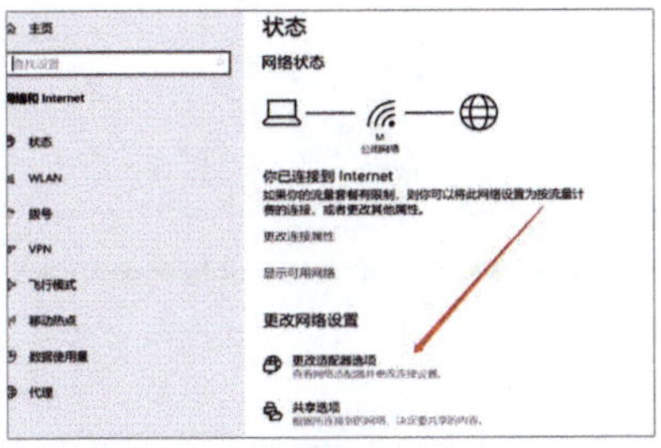

diǎnjī "wǎngluò", zhǎodào "wǎngluò hé gòngxiǎng zhōngxīn"

点击 "网络", 找到 "网络 和 共享 中心"

click "Network" to find "Network and Sharing Center"

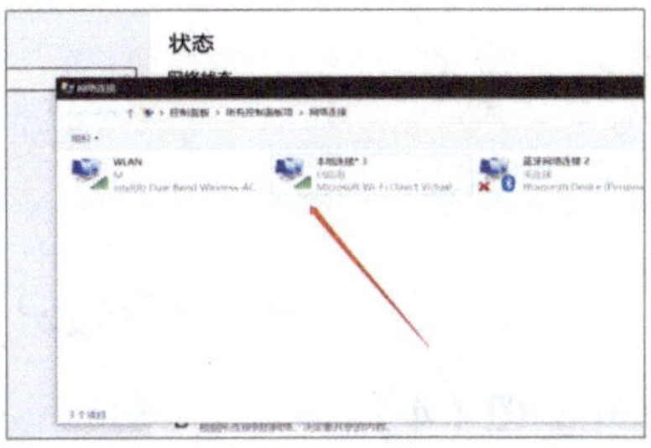

diǎnjī "wǎngluò hé gòngxiǎng zhōngxīn", zhǎodào "yǐtàiwǎng"

点击 "网络 和 共享 中心", 找到 "以太网"

click "Network and Sharing Center" to find "Ethernet"

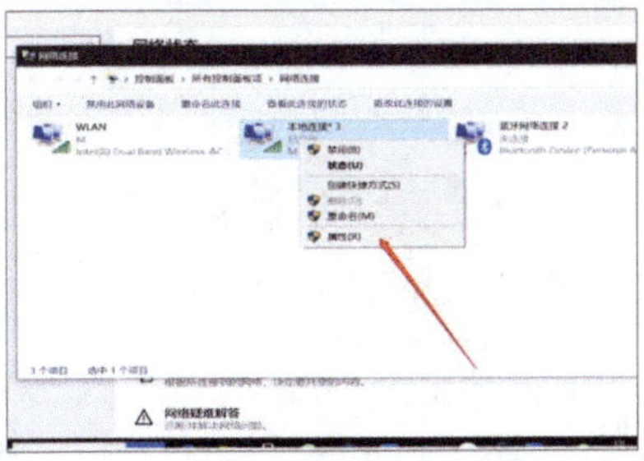

diǎnjī "yǐtàiwǎng", dédào "yǐtàiwǎng zhuàngtài", diǎnjī xiàfāng "shǔxìng", zhǎodào "Internet xiéyì bǎnběn 4 (TCP/IPv4)"

点击 "以太网", 得到 "以太网 状态", 点击 下方 "属性", 找到 "Internet 协议 版本 4 (TCP/IPv4)"

click "Ethernet" to get "Ethernet Status", then click "Properties" at the bottom of the drop-down box to find "Internet Protocol version 4 (TCP/IPv4)"

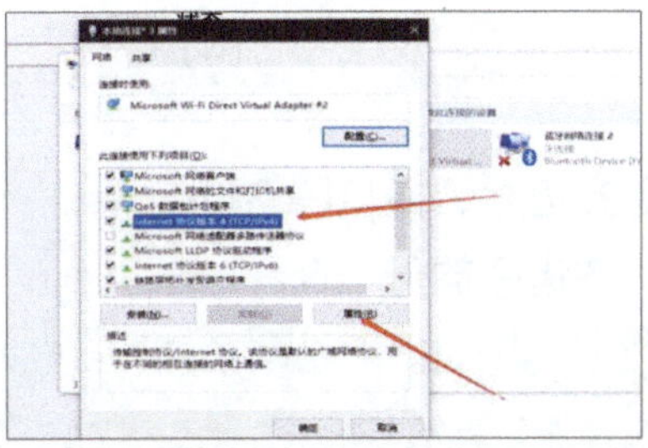

diǎnjī "Internet xiéyì bǎnběn 4 (TCP/IPv4)" xiàfāng "shǔxìng"

点击 "Internet 协议 版本 4 (TCP/IPv4)" 下方 "属性"

click "Properties" at the bottom of the window of "Internet Protocol version 4 (TCP/IPv4)"

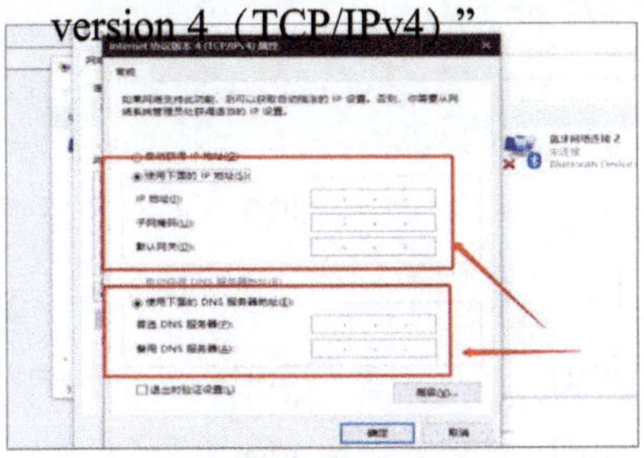

shèzhì jìngtài IP dìzhǐ

设置 静态 IP 地址

set the static IP address

题解 Introduction

1. 学习内容：网络地址的分类、范围和运用场所。
   Learning content: The classification, ranges and application scenarios of network addresses.
2. 知识目标：掌握 j、q、x 等声母及齐齿呼、撮口呼韵母的发音，掌握与网络地址相关的核心词语及表达。
   Knowledge target: Learn the pronunciation of the initials j, q, x, the even-teeth finals and the round-mouth finals; master the key words and expressions related to the network address.
3. 技能目标：掌握静态 IP 地址的设置。
   Skill target: Master the method of setting the static IP address.

第一部分 Part 1

语音 Phonetic Learning

一、语音知识 yǔyīn zhīshi Knowledge about Phonetics

声母和韵母（4） **Initials and finals (4)**

（1）声母 Initials：j q x

声母 Initial	国际音标 International Phonetic Alphabet	声母 Initial	国际音标 International Phonetic Alphabet	声母 Initial	国际音标 International Phonetic Alphabet
j	[tɕ]	q	[tɕʰ]	x	[ɕ]

（2）齐齿呼、撮口呼韵母 Even-teeth finals and round-mouth finals

齐齿呼韵母 Even-teeth finals

齐齿呼韵母 Even-teeth final	国际音标 International Phonetic Alphabet	齐齿呼韵母 Even-teeth finals	国际音标 International Phonetic Alphabet	齐齿呼韵母 Even-teeth finals	国际音标 International Phonetic Alphabet
i	[i]	ia	[iA]	ian	[iɛn]
		ie	[iɛ]	in	[in]
		iao	[iau]	iang	[iaŋ]
		iou	[iou]	ing	[iŋ]

撮口呼韵母 Round-mouth finals

撮口呼韵母 Round-mouth final	国际音标 International Phonetic Alphabet	撮口呼韵母 Round-mouth final	国际音标 International Phonetic Alphabet	撮口呼韵母 Round-mouth finals	国际音标 International Phonetic Alphabet
ü	[y]	üe	[yɛ]	üan	[yan]
				ün	[yn]
				iong	[yŋ]

二、语音练习 yǔyīn liànxí Phonetic Exercises

1. 听读辨音 Listen, read and discriminate the pronunciations. 04-01

j—zh	q—ch	x—sh
ju—zhu	qu—chu	xu—shu
ji—zhi	qi—chi	xi—shi
jie—zhe	qian—chan	xian—shan
jia—zha	qiao—chao	xie—she
jin—zhen	qin—chen	xing—sheng
jiu—zhou	qing—cheng	xiang—shang

2. 听读辨调 Listen, read and discriminate the tones. 04-02

yuè—yuē	jiā—jià	qī—qǐ	xué—xuè
yǔ—yú	jiǔ—jiù	qián—qiǎn	xī—xǐ
yīng—yǐng	jīn—jǐn	qù—qǔ	xiè—xiě
yòu—yǒu	jìng—jīng	qǐng—qīng	xíng—xìng
yān—yán	jiāng—jiàng	qiū—qiú	xiǎo—xiào

3. 读一读 Let's read.

① IP dìzhǐ IP 地址	② A lèi dìzhǐ A 类 地址	③ B lèi dìzhǐ B 类 地址	④ C lèi dìzhǐ C 类 地址
⑤ yǐtàiwǎng 以太网	⑥ tǐxì 体系	⑦ jiégòu 结构	⑧ shèzhì 设置
⑨ shǔxìng 属性	⑩ júyùwǎng 局域网	⑪ yígòng 一共	⑫ wǔ 五

第二部分 Part 2

课文 Texts

一、热身 rèshēn Warm-up

1. 给词语选择对应的图片。 **Match the pictures with corresponding words.**

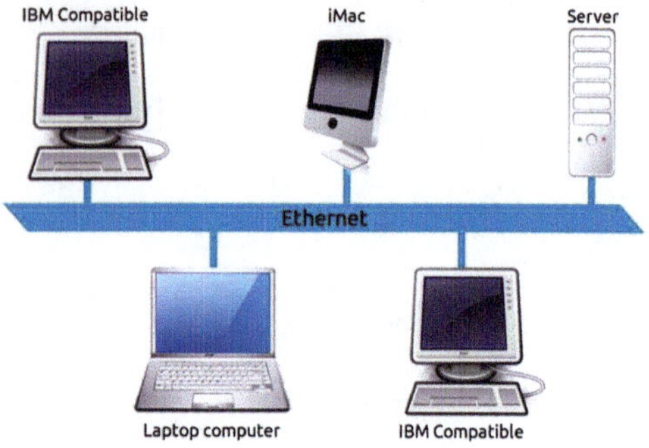

A.

B.

C.

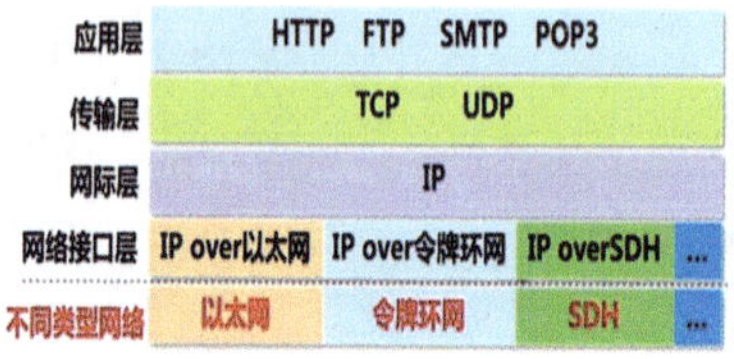

D.

wǎngluò
① 网络 ____________
network

IP dìzhǐ
② IP 地址 ____________
IP address

yǐtàiwǎng
③ 以太网 ____________
Ethernet

TCP/IP tǐxì jiégòu
④ TCP/IP 体系结构 ____________
TCP/IP architecture

2. 观看介绍网络地址设置的视频，并根据这些词在视频中出现的先后顺序，把相应的选项填入合适的空格。
Watch the video about the method of setting the network address, and fill in the blanks with corresponding options according to the order that the words appear in the video.

IP shèzhì A. IP 设置 setting the IP address	yǐtàiwǎng B. 以太网 ethernet	wǎngluò C. 网络 network	shǔxìng D. 属性 property

① ________ → ② ________ → ③ ________ → ④ ________

二、课文 kèwén Texts

A 04-03

shīfu: IP dìzhǐ yígòng yǒu A、B、C、D、E wǔ zhǒng lèixíng.
师傅：IP 地址一共有 A、B、C、D、E 五种类型。

túdì: Cháng yòng de IP dìzhǐ yǒu nǎ jǐ zhǒng lèixíng?
徒弟：常用的 IP 地址有哪几种类型？

shīfu: Cháng yòng de IP dìzhǐ yǒu A、B、C sān lèi.
师傅：常用的 IP 地址有 A、B、C 三类。

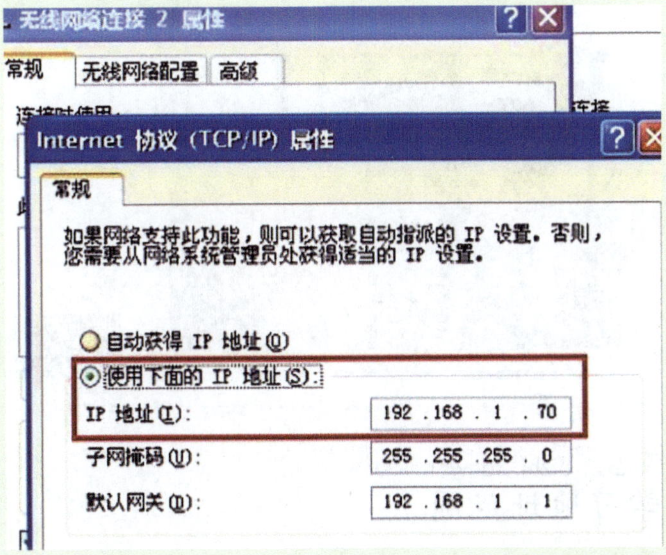

译文 yìwén Text in English

Master: There are five classes of IP addresses altogether: A, B, C, D and E.
Apprentice: What are the common classes of IP addresses?
Master: The common classes are A, B and C.

普通词语 pǔtōng cíyǔ General Vocabulary

04-04

1.	一共	yígòng	adv.	altogether
2.	五	wǔ	num.	five
3.	种	zhǒng	m.	type, kind
4.	类型	lèixíng	n.	type
5.	常用	cháng yòng	phr.	common
6.	哪	nǎ	pron.	which
7.	几	jǐ	pron.	several
8.	三	sān	num.	three
9.	类	lèi	m.	type

专业词语 zhuānyè cíyǔ Specialized Vocabulary

04-05

1.	IP 地址	IP dìzhǐ	phr.	IP address

B

04-06

shīfu: Jīntiān wǒmen xuéxí dìzhǐ fànwéi.
师傅：今天我们学习地址范围。

túdì: Shīfu, A lèi dìzhǐ fànwéi shì duōshao?
徒弟：师傅，A 类地址范围是多少？

shīfu: A lèi dìzhǐ fànwéi wéi 1.0.0.0 ～ 126.255.255.255.
师傅：A 类地址 范围 为 1.0.0.0 ～ 126.255.255.255。

túdì: B lèi dìzhǐ fànwéi ne?
徒弟：B 类地址范围呢？

shīfu: B lèi dìzhǐ fànwéi wéi 128.0.0.0 ～ 191.255.255.255.
师傅：B 类地址范围为 128.0.0.0 ～ 191.255.255.255。

túdì: C lèi ne?
徒弟：C 类呢？

shīfu: C lèi dìzhǐ fànwéi wéi 192.0.0.0 ～ 223.255.255.255.
师傅：C 类地址范围为 192.0.0.0 ～ 223.255.255.255。

译文 yìwén Text in English

Master: We're going to learn the address ranges today.
Apprentice: Master, what is the range of Class A addresses?
Master: The range is 1.0.0.0-126.255.255.255.
Apprentice: How about Class B addresses?
Master: The range is 128.0.0.0-191.255.255.255.
Apprentice: How about Class C addresses?
Master: The range is 192.0.0.0-223.255.255.255.

普通词语 pǔtōng cíyǔ General Vocabulary

04-07

1.	今天	jīntiān	n.	today
2.	我们	wǒmen	pron.	we, us
3.	学习	xuéxí	v.	learn, study
4.	范围	fànwéi	n.	range
5.	多少	duōshao	pron.	how many, how much
6.	为	wéi	v.	be

专业词语 zhuānyè cíyǔ Specialized Vocabulary

04-08

1.	A 类地址	A lèi dìzhǐ	phr.	Class A address
2.	B 类地址	B lèi dìzhǐ	phr.	Class B address
3.	C 类地址	C lèi dìzhǐ	phr.	Class C address

三、视听说 shì-tīng-shuō Viewing, Listening & Speaking

1. 观看介绍网络地址的视频，将它们与其适用的网络连线。

Watch the video about the network address, and match the addresses with suitable networks.

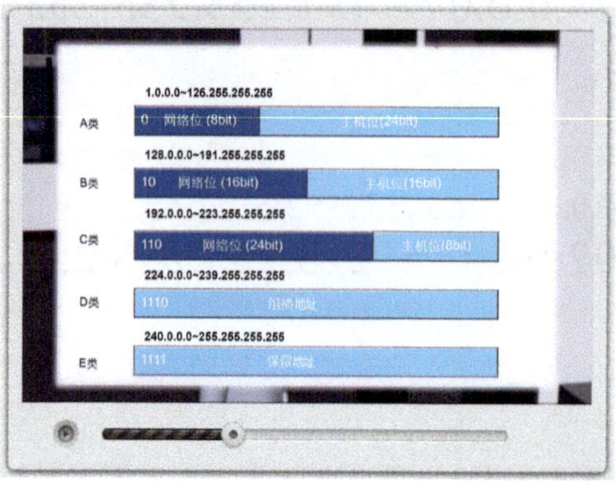

A lèi dìzhǐ ① A 类地址 Class A address	zhōngxíng wǎngluò A. 中 型 网 络 medium-sized network
B lèi dìzhǐ ② B 类地址 Class B address	júyù wǎngluò B. 局域 网络 local area network
C lèi dìzhǐ ③ C 类地址 Class C address	dàxíng wǎngluò C. 大型 网络 large-scale network

2. 说一说 **Let's talk.**

请模仿说出 A、B、C 三类地址适用的网络。

Please talk about the networks the three classes of network addresses are fit for respectively.

四、学以致用 xuéyǐzhìyòng Practicing What You Have Learnt

1. 观看介绍网络地址的使用场所的视频，将网络地址与其对应的使用场所连线。

Watch the the video about the application scenarios of network addresses, and match the network addresses with the corresponding scenarios.

A.

B.

C.

1. dàxíng wǎngluò 大型 网络 large-scale network
2. zhōngxíng wǎngluò 中型 网络 medium-sized network
3. júyùwǎng 局域网 local area network

补充专业词语 bǔchōng zhuānyè cíyǔ Supplementary Specialized Vocabulary

04-09

1.	以太网	yǐtàiwǎng	n.	Ethernet
2.	体系	tǐxì	n.	system
3.	结构	jiégòu	n.	structure
4.	设置	shèzhì	v.	set
5.	属性	shǔxìng	n.	property
6.	局域网	júyùwǎng	n.	local area network

第三部分 Part 3

课堂用语 *Classroom Expressions*

1. 准备好了吗？ Zhǔnbèi hǎo le ma? Are you ready?
2. 请打开书，翻到第十页。Qǐng dǎkāi shū, fāndào dì-shí yè. Open your book and turn to Page 10.

第四部分 Part 4

单元实训 *Unit Practical Training*

静态 IP 地址的设置 Jìngtài IP dìzhǐ de shèzhì Setting the Static IP Address

实训目的 Training purpose

掌握静态 IP 地址的设置步骤和方法。

Master the steps and methods of setting the static IP address.

实训内容 Training content

静态 IP 地址的设置。

Setting the static IP address.

实训组织 Training organization

每组 3 ～ 5 人。选出一个组长。

Students work in groups of 3-5. Each group chooses a group leader.

实训步骤 Training steps

1. 通过跟读、图片展示及小组比赛等方法复习巩固 IP 地址设置的步骤名称。
   Review and consolidate name of the steps of setting an IP address through listening and repeating, picture presentation, group Q&A quiz and other methods.
2. 点击“网络”，找到“网络和共享中心”。
   Click “Network” to find “Network and Sharing Center”.
3. 点击“网络和共享中心”，找到“以太网”。
   Click “Network and Sharing Center” to find “Ethernet”.
4. 点击“以太网”，得到“以太网状态”，点击下方“属性”，找到“Internet 协议版本 4（TCP/IPv4）”。
   Click “Ethernet” to get “Ethernet Status”, then click “Properties” at the bottom of the drop-down box to find “Internet Protocol version 4 (TCP/IPv4)”.
5. 点击“Internet 协议版本 4（TCP/IPv4）”下方“属性”。
   Click “Properties” under “Internet Protocol version 4 (TCP/IPv4)”.
6. 设置静态 IP 地址。
   Set the static IP address.
7. 学员总结，教师总评。
   The trainees make a summary and the teacher comments on the training.

第五部分 Part 5

单元小结 Unit Summary

cíyǔ
词语
Vocabulary

普通词语 General Vocabulary

1.	一共	yígòng	adv.	altogether
2.	五	wǔ	num.	five
3.	种	zhǒng	m.	type, kind
4.	类型	lèixíng	n.	type

cíyǔ
词语
Vocabulary

5.	常用	cháng yòng	phr.	common
6.	哪	nǎ	pron.	which
7.	几	jǐ	pron.	several
8.	三	sān	num.	three
9.	类	lèi	m.	type
10.	今天	jīntiān	n.	today
11.	我们	wǒmen	pron.	we, us
12.	学习	xuéxí	v.	learn, study
13.	范围	fànwéi	n.	range
14.	多少	duōshao	pron.	how many, how much
15.	为	wéi	v.	be

专业词语 Specialized Vocabulary

1.	IP 地址	IP dìzhǐ	phr.	IP address
2.	A 类地址	A lèi dìzhǐ	phr.	Class A address
3.	B 类地址	B lèi dìzhǐ	phr.	Class B address
4.	C 类地址	C lèi dìzhǐ	phr.	Class C address

补充专业词语 Supplementary Specialized Vocabulary

1.	以太网	yǐtàiwǎng	n.	Ethernet
2.	体系	tǐxì	n.	system
3.	结构	jiégòu	n.	structure
4.	设置	shèzhì	v.	set
5.	属性	shǔxìng	n.	property
6.	局域网	júyùwǎng	n.	local area network

jùzi
句子
Sentences

1. IP 地址一共有 A、B、C、D、E 五种类型。
2. 常用的 IP 地址是 A、B、C 三类。
3. A 类地址范围为 1.0.0.0 ～ 126.255.255.255，B 类地址范围为 128.0.0.0 ～ 191.255.255.255，C 类地址范围为 192.0.0.0 ～ 223.255.255.255。

5

Kuāndài shàngwǎng

宽带上网

Broadband Internet Access

ānzhuāng kuāndài wǎngluò

安装 宽带 网络

Installing Broadband Network

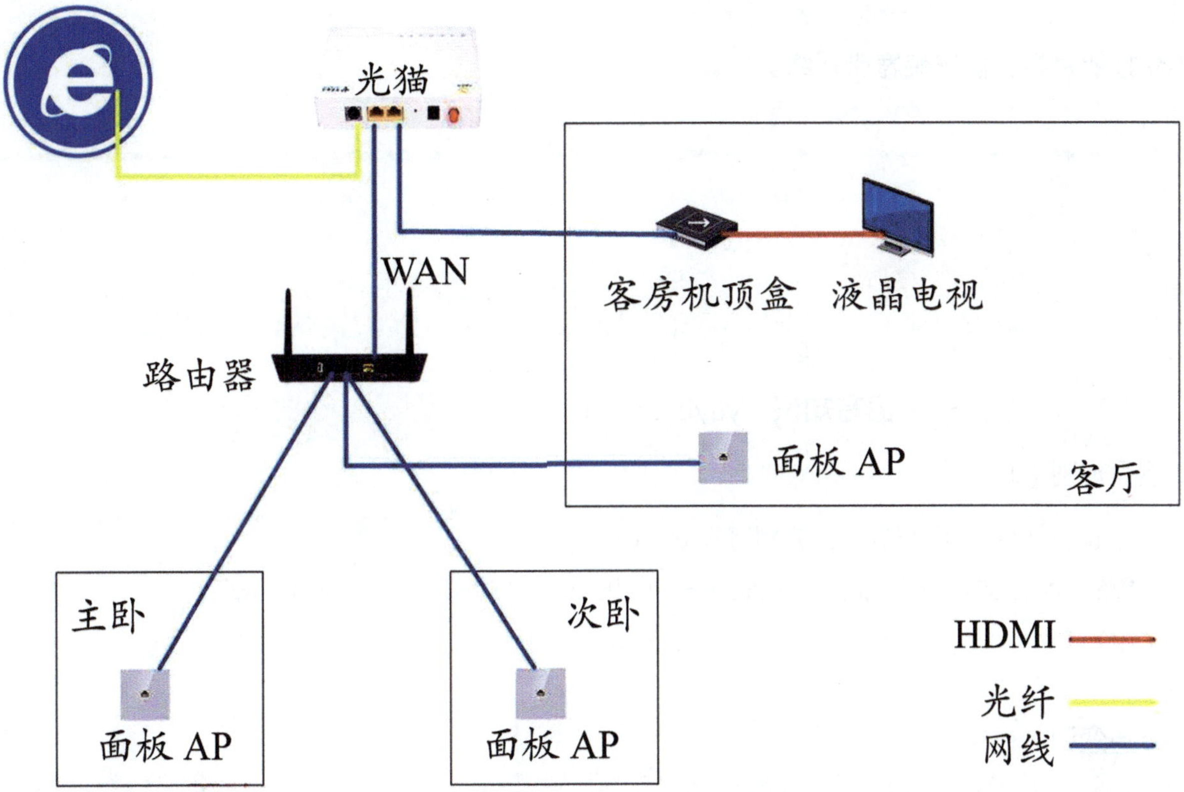

jiāng rùhù guāngxiān liánrù guāngmāo

1. 将入户 光纤 连入 光猫

connect the FTTH (fiber-to-the-home) cable to the optical modem

jiāng kuāndài lùyóuqì liánjiē dào guāngmāo

2. 将 宽带路由器连接到 光猫

connect the broadband router to the optical modem

jiǎnchá guāngmāo yǔ kuāndài lùyóuqì de liánjiē

3. 检查 光猫 与宽带路由器的连接

check the connection between the optical modem and the broadband router

pèizhì kuāndài lùyóuqì

4. 配置宽带路由器

configure the broadband router

题解 Introduction

1. 学习内容：宽带上网所需材料和基本操作步骤。
   Learning content: The materials and basic operation steps needed for broadband Internet access.
2. 知识目标：学习 i、u、ü 单独构成音节时的拼写规则、三声变调和"不"的变调，学习与宽带上网相关的核心词语与表达。
   Knowledge target: Learn the spelling rules of "i", "u" and "ü" as independent syllables by themselves, the third-tone sandhi, and the tone sandhi of "不"; master the key words and expressions related to broadband Internet access.
3. 技能目标：能安装宽带网络。
   Skill target: Be able to set up a broadband network.

第一部分 Part 1

语音 Phonetic Learning

一、语音知识 yǔyīn zhīshi Knowledge about Phonetics

1. 拼写规则（1） Spelling rules (1)

i、u、ü 单独构成音节时，分别写作 yi、wu、yu。

When "i", "u" or "ü" makes a syllable by itself, the syllable is written as follows.

i → yi　　u → wu　　ü → yu

2. 三声变调 Third-tone sandhi

两个三声音节连读时，前一个三声声调读二声。例如：

When a third-tone syllable is followed by another third-tone syllable, the third tone in the first syllable is pronounced as the second tone. For example,

nǐ hǎo 读作 ní hǎo　　Fǎyǔ 读作 Fáyǔ

3. "不"的变调 Tone sandhi of "不"

"不"（bù）本调是第四声。"不"在第一声、第二声、第三声前面时，声调不变；在第四声前面时，读第二声。例如：

"不 (bù)" is a fourth-tone syllable by itself. The tone doesn't change when "不 (bù)" is followed by a first-tone, second-tone or third-tone syllable, but it becomes the second tone when "不 (bù)" is followed by a fourth-tone syllable. For example,

不 bù + { 吃 chī / 来 lái / 好 hǎo / 是 shì } = { 不＋吃 bù chī / 不＋来 bù lái / 不＋好 bù hǎo / 不＋是 bú shì }

二、语音练习 yǔyīn liànxí Phonetic Exercises

1. 读下面的词语，并在“u”上边标上声调。 **Read the following words and add tone marks above “u”.**

不喝 bu hē	不吃 bu chī	不多 bu duō
不学 bu xué	不想 bu xiǎng	不小 bu xiǎo
不买 bu mǎi	不看 bu kàn	不去 bu qù
不对 bu duì	不累 bu lèi	不要 bu yào
不漂亮 bu piàoliang	不客气 bu kèqi	不上网 bu shàngwǎng
不新鲜 bu xīnxiān	不知道 bu zhīdào	不开门 bu kāimén

2. 读一读 **Let’s read.**

① 宽带 kuāndài	② 光猫 guāngmāo	③ 冷接子 lěngjiēzǐ	④ 网线 wǎngxiàn
⑤ 入户 rùhù	⑥ 光纤 guāngxiān	⑦ 光口 guāngkǒu	⑧ 电源线 diànyuánxiàn
⑨ 对接 duìjiē	⑩ 转换 zhuǎnhuàn	⑪ 信号 xìnhào	⑫ 广域网 guǎngyùwǎng

第二部分 Part 2

课文 Texts

一、热身 rèshēn Warm-up

1. 给词语选择对应的图片。 **Match the pictures with corresponding words.**

A.

B.

C.

D.

① 宽带路由器 kuāndài lùyóuqì ____________
broadband router

② 光纤冷接子 guāngxiān lěngjiēzǐ ____________
fiber-optic cold connector

③ guāngxiàn 光纤 ________ optical fiber

④ guāngmāo 光猫 ________ optical modem

2. 观看介绍光纤、光猫和冷接子的作用的视频，并把它们与其作用连线。

Watch the video about the functions of the optical fiber, optical modem and cold connector, and match them with their functions.

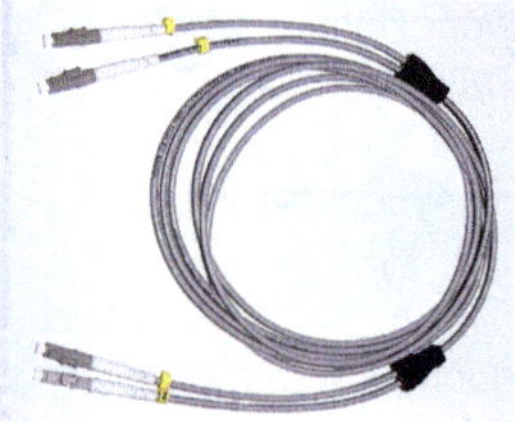

A.

B.

C.

① guāngxiān duìjiē 光纤 对接 optical fiber butt-coupling

② zhuǎnhuàn xìnhào 转换 信号 signal conversion

③ chuánshū guāngxìnhào 传输 光信号 optical signal transmission

二、课文 kèwén Texts

A 05-01

shīfu: Nǐ jīntiān hěn máng ma?

师傅：你今天很忙吗？

túdì: Shì de, hěn máng. Wǒ yào xuéxí rúhé ānzhuāng kuāndài.
徒弟：是的，很忙。我要学习如何安装宽带。

shīfu: Ānzhuāng kuāndài xūyào shénme cáiliào, nǐ zhīdào ma?
师傅：安装宽带需要什么材料，你知道吗？

túdì: Xūyào guāngxiān、guāngmāo、kuāndài lùyóuqì、guāngxiān lěngjiēzǐ、yǐtàiwǎng wǎngxiàn hé RJ45 shuǐjīngtóu.
徒弟：需要光纤、光猫、宽带路由器、光纤冷接子、以太网网线和 RJ45 水晶头。

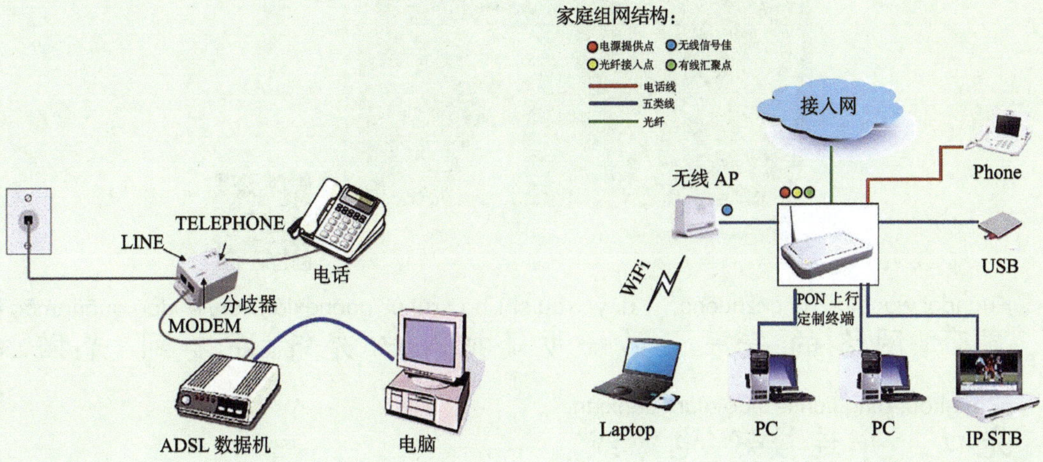

译文 yìwén Text in English

Master: Are you busy today?

Apprentice: Yes, very busy. I'm going to learn how to install broadband.

Master: Do you know what materials are needed to install broadband?

Apprentice: Optical fiber, optical modem, broadband router, fiber-optic cold connector, Ethernet cable and RJ45 plug.

普通词语 pǔtōng cíyǔ General Vocabulary

05-02

1.	你	nǐ	pron.	you
2.	很	hěn	adv.	very
3.	忙	máng	adj.	busy
4.	吗	ma	part.	*used at the end of a yes/no question*
5.	我	wǒ	pron.	I, me
6.	要	yào	aux.	be going to
7.	如何	rúhé	pron.	what way
8.	安装	ānzhuāng	v.	install
9.	材料	cáiliào	n.	material
10.	知道	zhīdào	v.	know

专业词语 zhuānyè cíyǔ Specialized Vocabulary

05-03

1.	宽带	kuāndài	n.	broadband
2.	光猫	guāngmāo	n.	optical modem
3.	冷接子	lěngjiēzǐ	n.	cold connector
4.	网线	wǎngxiàn	n.	network cable

B 05-04

shīfu: Kuāndài wǎngluò de ānzhuāng, dì-yī bù shì bǎ rùhù guāngxiān liánjiē dào guāngmāo de guāngkǒu, bìng liánjiē hǎo diànyuánxiàn.

师傅：宽带网络的安装，第一步是把入户光纤连接到光猫的光口，并连接好电源线。

túdì: Xià yí bù ne?

徒弟：下一步呢？

shīfu: Bǎ kuāndài lùyóuqì yòng wǎngxiàn liánjiē dào guāngmāo, bìng liánjiē hǎo diànyuánxiàn.

师傅：把宽带路由器用网线连接到光猫，并连接好电源线。

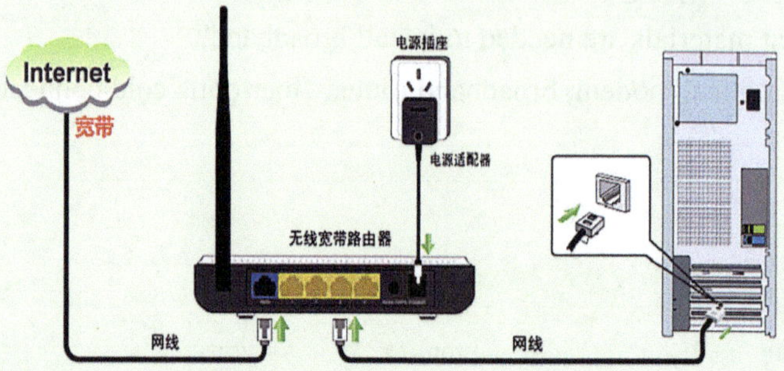

译文 yìwén Text in English

Master: When installing the broadband network, the first step is to connect the FTTH cable to the optical port of the optical modem and connect the power cord properly.

Apprentice: What's the next step?

Master: Connect the broadband router to the optical modem with the network cable, and connect the power cord properly.

普通词语 pǔtōng cíyǔ General Vocabulary

05-05

1.	第一步	dì-yī bù	phr.	first step
	第一	dì-yī	num.	first
	步	bù	n.	step
2.	把	bǎ	prep.	*used in the sentence pattern "Subject + 把 + Object + Verb +..."*
3.	到	dào	v.	get to
4.	并	bìng	conj.	and
5.	好	hǎo	adj.	well
6.	下一步	xià yí bù	phr.	next step
	下	xià	n.	next
7.	用	yòng	prep.	with

专业词语 zhuānyè cíyǔ Specialized Vocabulary

05-06

1.	入户光纤	rùhù guāngxiān	phr.	in-building optical fiber
2.	光口	guāngkǒu	n.	optical port
3.	电源线	diànyuánxiàn	n.	power cord

三、视听说 shì-tīng-shuō Viewing, Listening & Speaking

1. 观看介绍以太网的视频，并选出正确答案。

Watch the video about the Ethernet and choose the correct answers.

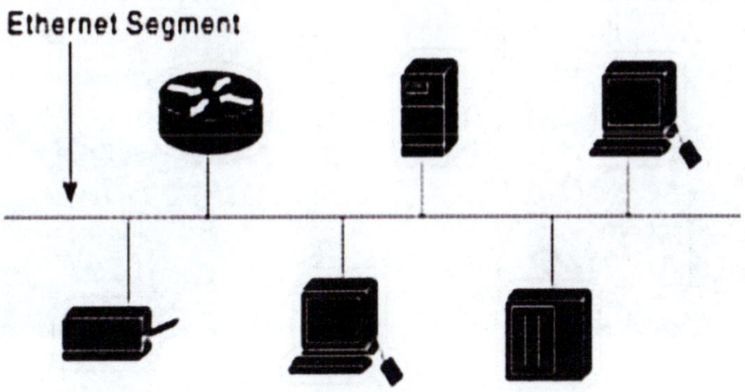

Guānyú yǐtàiwǎng， zhèngquè de shì:
关于以太网，正确的是：________。
About the Ethernet, the correct descriptions are:

shì guǎngyùwǎng
A. 是广域网
It's a wide area network.

zhǐ néng yǒu yí gè yǐtàiwǎng
B. 只能有一个以太网
We can only have one Ethernet.

shì júyùwǎng
C. 是局域网
It's a local area network.

xū zài yídìng de jùlí zhī nèi
D. 需在一定的距离之内
It's limited to a certain distance.

2. 说一说 **Let's talk.**

请说说以太网和因特网有什么不同。

Please talk about the differences between the Ethernet and the Internet.

四、学以致用 xuéyǐzhìyòng Practicing What You Have Learnt

观看介绍局域网的视频，在下列图片中选出局域网能覆盖其整个范围的选项。

Watch the video about the local area network, and select the areas that can be fully covered by the local area network from the following pictures.

A.

B.

C.

D.

E.

F.

Júyùwǎng néng fùgài qí zhěnggè fànwéi de xuǎnxiàng shì:
局域网能覆盖其整个范围的选项是：__________________。
The areas that can be fully covered by a local area network are:

补充专业词语 bǔchōng zhuānyè cíyǔ Supplementary Specialized Vocabulary

05-07

1.	对接	duìjiē	v.	butt-couple, splice
2.	转换	zhuǎnhuàn	v.	convert
3.	信号	xìnhào	n.	signal
4.	广域网	guǎngyùwǎng	n.	wide area network

第三部分 Part 3

课堂用语 Classroom Expressions

1. 我明白了。Wǒ míngbai le. I see/understand.
2. 我不懂。Wǒ bù dǒng. I don't know/understand.

第四部分 Part 4

单元实训 Unit Practical Training

安装宽带网络 ānzhuāng kuāndài wǎngluò Installing Broadband Network

实训目的 Training purpose

了解并掌握宽带网络的安装步骤和方法，培养团队合作与竞争意识，提高动手操作能力和汉语沟通能力。

Learn about and master the steps and methods of installing broadband network, cultivate the spirit of teamwork and awareness of competition, and improve the hands-on ability and communication skills in Chinese.

实训组织 Training organization

每组 3～5 人，选出一名组长。

Students work in groups of 3-5. Each group chooses a group leader.

实训内容 Training content

宽带网络的安装

Broadband network installation

实训步骤 Training steps

1. 各小组组长检查组内各成员的安装材料准备情况，确保材料齐备。
   Each group leader checks the installation materials prepared by each group member to ensure that everything is ready.
2. 开始安装，之后进行配置。
   Start to install the broadband network and then configure the network.
3. 各小组成员检查自己的宽带安装及运行情况，并将问题汇报给小组组长。
   Each team member checks the installation and running situations of his or her broadband network, and report the problems to the group leader.

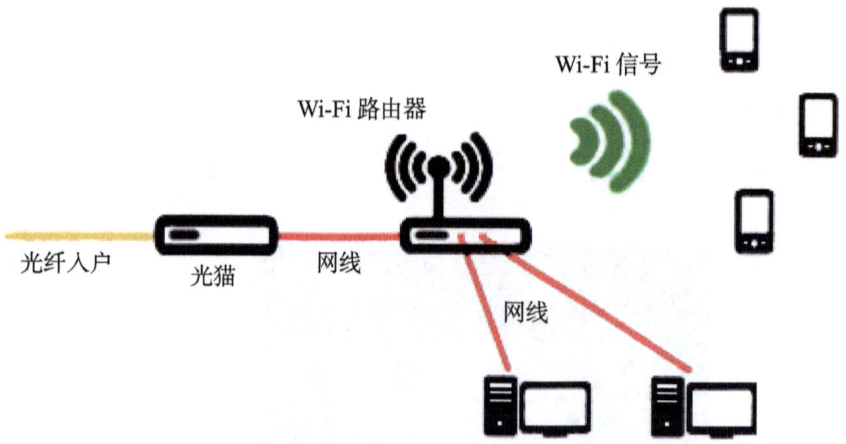

4. 各小组组长将情况及问题反馈给教师，在教师指导下进行必要的处置。
   The group leader of every group reports the situations and problems to the teacher, and take necessary action under the guidance of the teacher.
5. 实训结束，教师总结评价。
   The teacher makes a summary and comment at the end of the training.

第五部分 Part 5

单元小结 Unit Summary

cíyǔ
词语
Vocabulary

普通词语 General Vocabulary

1.	你	nǐ	pron.	you
2.	很	hěn	adv.	very
3.	忙	máng	adj.	busy
4.	吗	ma	part.	*used at the end of a yes/no question*
5.	我	wǒ	pron.	I, me
6.	要	yào	aux.	be going to
7.	如何	rúhé	pron.	what way
8.	安装	ānzhuāng	v.	install
9.	材料	cáiliào	n.	material
10.	知道	zhīdào	v.	know
11.	第一步	dì-yī bù	phr.	first step
	第一	dì-yī	num.	first
	步	bù	n.	step
12.	把	bǎ	prep.	*used in the sentence pattern "Subject + 把 + Object + Verb +..."*
13.	到	dào	v.	get to
14.	并	bìng	conj.	and
15.	好	hǎo	adj.	well
16.	下一步	xià yí bù	phr.	next step
	下	xià	n.	next
17.	用	yòng	prep.	with

专业词语 Specialized Vocabulary

1.	宽带	kuāndài	n.	broadband
2.	光猫	guāngmāo	n.	optical modem
3.	冷接子	lěngjiēzǐ	n.	cold connector
4.	网线	wǎngxiàn	n.	network cable
5.	入户光纤	rùhù guāngxiān	phr.	in-building optical fiber
6.	光口	guāngkǒu	n.	optical port
7.	电源线	diànyuánxiàn	n.	power cord

cíyǔ 词语 Vocabulary	补充专业词语 Supplementary Specialized Vocabulary			
	1. 对接	duìjiē	v.	butt-couple, splice
	2. 转换	zhuǎnhuàn	v.	convert
	3. 信号	xìnhào	n.	signal
	4. 广域网	guǎngyùwǎng	n.	wide area network

jùzi 句子 Sentences

1. 安装宽带需要光纤、光猫、宽带路由器、光纤冷接子、以太网网线和 RJ45 水晶头。
2. 第一步是把入户光纤连接到光猫的光口，并连接好电源线。
3. 下一步是把宽带路由器用网线连接到光猫，并连接好电源线。

6

Zǔjiàn wúxiàn wǎngluò

组建无线网络

Setting up a Wireless Network

ānzhuāng Huáwéi "zhìhuì shēnghuó" APP

安装 华为 "智慧 生活" APP

Installing the Huawei "AI Life" APP

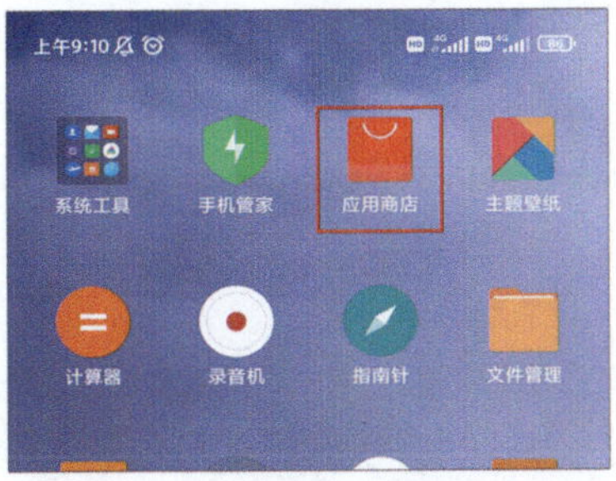

dǎkāi "yìngyòng shāngdiàn" APP

打开 "应用 商店" APP

open the "APP Store" APP

zài sōusuǒkuàng zhōng shūrù Hànzì "zhìhuì shēnghuó"

在 搜索框 中 输入汉字 "智慧 生活"

enter the Chinese characters "AI Life" in the search box

diǎnjī "sōusuǒ" ànniǔ

点击 "搜索" 按钮

click the "Search" button

zhǎodào "zhìhuì shēnghuó" APP, diǎnjī "ānzhuāng" ànniǔ

找到 "智慧 生活" APP，点击 "安装" 按钮

find the "AI Life" APP and click the "Install" button

diǎnjī "dǎkāi" ànniǔ

点击 "打开" 按钮

click the "Open" button

题解 Introduction

1. 学习内容：硬件和软件的基本知识，硬件和软件的安装步骤和方法。
   Learning content: The basic knowledge of hardware and software; the steps and methods of installing hardware and software.
2. 知识目标：掌握以"i""u""ü"开头的韵母自成音节时的拼写规则，掌握与组建无线网络相关的核心词语与表达。
   Knowledge target: Master the spelling rules when the finals starting with "i", "u" and "ü" form independent syllables; master the key words and expressions related to setting up a wireless network.
3. 技能目标：能够组建无线网络。
   Skill target: Be able to set up a wireless network.

第一部分 Part 1

语音 Phonetic Learning

一、语音知识 yǔyīn zhīshi Knowledge about Phonetics

拼写规则（2） Spelling rules (2)

（1）以"i"开头的韵母自成音节时，除了"in""ing"前加"y"外，其他均是把"i"写作"y"。

When "i" starts a syllable, it is written as "y", except in "in" and "ing", where "y" is added at the beginning.

ia→ya	ie→ye
iao→yao	iou→you
ian→yan	iang→yang
iong→yong	
in→yin	ing→ying

（2）以"u"开头的韵母自成音节时，"u"写作"w"。

When "u" starts a syllable, it is written as "w".

ua→wa	uo→wo
uai→wai	uei→wei
uan→wan	uen→wen
uang→wang	ueng→weng

（3）以"ü"开头的韵母自成音节时，"ü"前面加上"y"，去掉"ü"上的两点。

When "ü" starts a syllable, "y" is added in front of it and "ü" is written as "u".

üe→yue	üan→yuan	ün→yun

二、语音练习 yǔyīn liànxí Phonetic Exercises

读一读 Let's read.

① yìngjiàn 硬件　② ruǎnjiàn 软件　③ ānzhuāngbāo 安装包　④ sǎomiáo 扫描

èrwéimǎ ⑤ 二维码	xiàzài ⑥ 下载	zhìhuì ⑦ 智慧	shēnghuó ⑧ 生活
sōusuǒ ⑨ 搜索	chuānqiángxìng ⑩ 穿墙性	fùgài ⑪ 覆盖	qūyù ⑫ 区域

第二部分　Part 2

课文　Texts

一、热身　rèshēn　Warm-up

1. 给词语选择对应的图片。　Match the pictures with corresponding words.

A.

B.

C.

D.

Huáwéi APP ① 华为 APP ________ Huawei APP	zǐmǔ lùyóuqì ② 子母路由器 ________ master router and sub-router
diànyuánxiàn ③ 电源线 ________ power cord	shǒujī ④ 手机 ________ mobile phone

2. 观看介绍华为“智慧生活”APP 安装流程的视频，并根据正确的流程顺序填空。
Watch the video of the process of installing the Huawei “AI Life” APP, and fill in the blanks with the correct order of the installing process.

A.

B.

C.

D.

E.

Ānzhuāng Huáwéi “zhìhuì shēnghuó” APP de liúchéng shì:
安装 华为“智慧 生活”APP 的 流程 是：
The process of installing Huawei “AI Life” APP is:

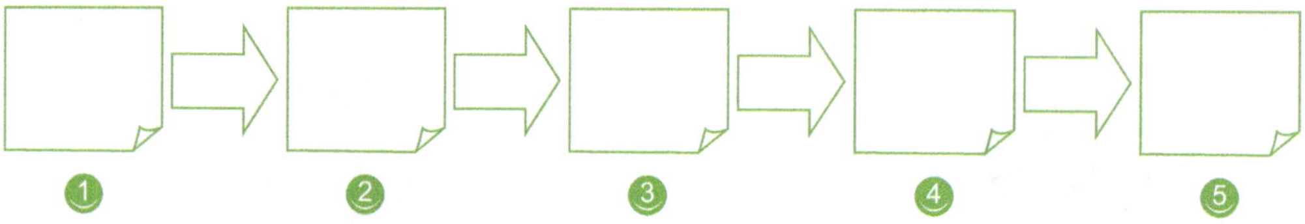

二、课文 kèwén Texts

A 06-01

túdì: Shīfu, qǐngwèn jīntiān yǒu shénme ānpái?
徒弟：师傅，请问今天 有 什么安排？

shīfu: Xuéxí yìngjiàn hé ruǎnjiàn de ānzhuāng.
师傅：学习硬件和软件的安装。

túdì: Qǐngwèn shénme shì yìngjiàn? Shénme shì ruǎnjiàn?
徒弟：请问 什么 是 硬件？什么 是 软件？

shīfu: Néng kàndejiàn, mōdezháo de jiù shì yìngjiàn, shǒujī lǐmiàn ānzhuāng de ānzhuāngbāo jiù shì ruǎnjiàn.
师傅：能看得见、摸得着的就是硬件，手机里面安装的安装包就是软件。

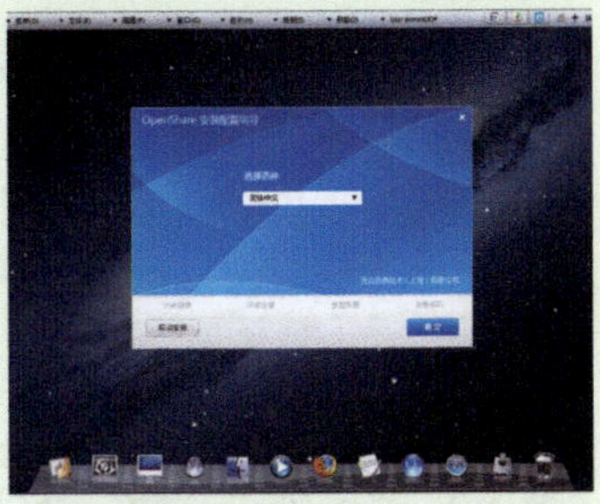

译文 yìwén Text in English

Apprentice: Master, what are we going to do today?
Master: To learn how to install the hardware and software.
Apprentice: What is hardware and what is software?
Master: What you can see and touch is hardware, and the installation packages installed in the mobile phone are software.

普通词语 pǔtōng cíyǔ General Vocabulary

06-02

1.	安排	ānpái	n./v.	plan; arrange
2.	能	néng	aux.	can
3.	看得见	kàndejiàn	v.	can be seen, be visible
4.	摸得着	mōdezháo	phr.	can be touched, be tangible
5.	就	jiù	adv.	just, exactly
6.	手机	shǒujī	n.	mobile phone
7.	里面	lǐmiàn	n.	inside

专业词语 zhuānyè cíyǔ Specialized Vocabulary

06-03

1.	硬件	yìngjiàn	n.	hardware
2.	软件	ruǎnjiàn	n.	software
3.	安装包	ānzhuāngbāo	n.	installation package

B 06-04

túdì: Shīfu, qǐngwèn yìngjiàn rúhé ānzhuāng?
徒弟：师傅，请问 硬件如何 安装？

shīfu: Liánjiē wǎngxiàn hé diànyuán.
师傅：连接 网线 和 电源。

túdì: Ruǎnjiàn rúhé ānzhuāng?
徒弟：软件 如何安装？

shīfu: Shǒujī sǎomiáo èrwéimǎ, xiàzài bìng ānzhuāng, lìrú Huáwéi “zhìhuì shēnghuó” APP.
师傅：手机扫描二维码，下载并 安装，例如 华为 “智慧 生活” APP。

译文 yìwén Text in English

Apprentice: Master, how do I install the hardware?
Master: Connect the network cable and power supply.
Apprentice: How do I install the software?
Master: Scan the QR code with your mobile, download and install it, for example, Huawei “AI Life” APP.

普通词语 pǔtōng cíyǔ General Vocabulary

06-05

1.	华为	Huáwéi	pn.	Huawei

专业词语 zhuānyè cíyǔ Specialized Vocabulary

06-06

1.	扫描	sǎomiáo	v.	scan
2.	二维码	èrwéimǎ	n.	QR code
3.	下载	xiàzài	v.	download
4.	智慧生活	zhìhuì shēnghuó	phr.	AI Life
	智慧	zhìhuì	n.	wisdom, intelligence
	生活	shēnghuó	n.	life

三、视听说 shì-tīng-shuō Viewing, Listening & Speaking

1. 观看介绍无线网的视频，并把正确答案填在横线上。

Watch the video about Wi-Fi, and fill in the blanks with corresponding answers.

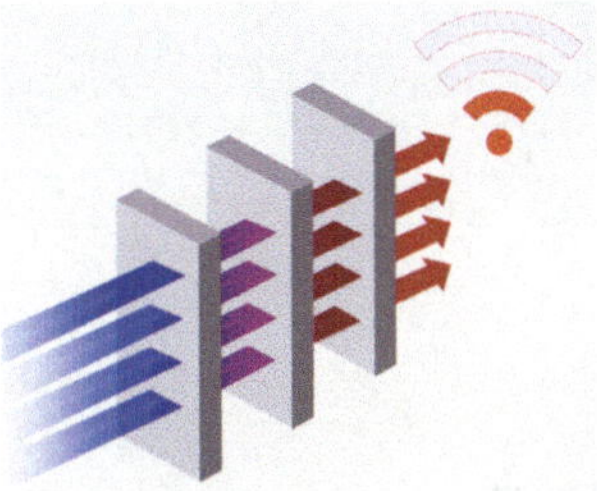

chuānqiángxìng ruò
A. 穿墙性弱
weak penetrability

yīngzài qí fùgài qūyù nèi
B. 应在其覆盖区域内
service available within its coverage area

xūyào mìmǎ
C. 需要密码
requiring password

kě shǐ duō gè yònghù liánjiē
D. 可使多个用户连接
supporting multiple users simultaneously

biànjié
E. 便捷
convenient

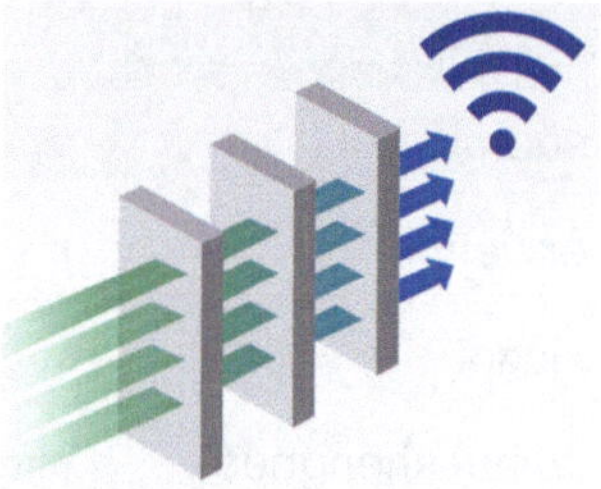

chuānqiángxìng qiáng
F. 穿墙性强
strong penetrability

Yǐshàng xuǎnxiàng zhōng, shǔyú wúxiànwǎng de tèdiǎn de shì:
以上选项中，属于无线网的特点的是：________________。
Among the above options, the characteristics of Wi-Fi are:

2. 说一说 Let's talk.

请说出无线网的特点。 Please speak out the characteristics of Wi-Fi.

四、学以致用 xuéyǐzhìyòng Practicing What You Have Learnt

观看介绍子母路由器的视频，并将选项 A 和 B 分别与对应的户型连线。

Watch the video about the master router and sub-router, and match the options A and B with corresponding houses respectively.

yí gè lùyóuqì jí kě
A. 一个路由器即可
One router is enough.

xūyào zǐmǔ lùyóuqì
B. 需要子母路由器
A master router and its sub-routers are needed.

①

②

补充专业词语 bǔchōng zhuānyè cíyǔ Supplementary Specialized Vocabulary

06-07

1.	搜索	sōusuǒ	v.	search
2.	穿墙性	chuānqiángxìng	n.	penetrability
3.	覆盖区域	fùgài qūyù	phr.	coverage area
4.	密码	mìmǎ	n.	password

第三部分 Part 3

课堂用语 Classroom Expressions

1. 现在做练习。Xiànzài zuò liànxí. Now it's time for exercises.
2. 周一交作业。Zhōuyī jiāo zuòyè. Hand in your homework on Monday.

第四部分 Part 4

单元实训 Unit Practical Training

配置无线网络 pèizhì wúxiàn wǎngluò Configuring a Wireless Network

实训目的 Training purpose

掌握安装子母路由器的步骤，并能独立完成安装，使计算机能够上网。

Master the steps of installing the master router and sub-router, and be able to complete the installation independently to connect the computer to the Internet.

实训组织 Training organization

每组 4 人，选出一个组长。

Students work in groups of 4. Each group chooses a group leader.

实训内容 Training content

安装子母路由器

Installing the master router and sub-router

实训步骤 Training steps

❶ 由组长首先清点安装需要的所有硬件，填入硬件清单。

The group leader checks all the hardware needed and list the names of the hardware.

❷ 每个人按步骤完成安装并进行配置：

Each group member completes the installation and configuration according to the installation steps:

1）连接硬件设备。

Connect the hardware devices.

2）打开“应用市场”，安装“智慧生活”APP。

Open the “APP Store” and install the “AI Life” APP.

3）打开“智慧生活”APP，点击“配置”按钮，进行手机端的配置。

Open the “AI Life” APP and click the “Configuration” button to start the configuration on the mobile phone.

❸ 学员总结，教师总评。

The students make a summary and the teacher comments on the training.

第五部分 Part 5

单元小结 Unit Summary

cíyǔ
词语
Vocabulary

普通词语 General Vocabulary

1.	安排	ānpái	n./v.	plan; arrange
2.	能	néng	aux.	can
3.	看得见	kàndejiàn	v.	can be seen, be visible
4.	摸得着	mōdezháo	phr.	can be touched, be tangible
5.	就	jiù	adv.	just, exactly
6.	手机	shǒujī	n.	mobile phone
7.	里面	lǐmiàn	n.	inside
8.	华为	Huáwéi	pn.	Huawei

专业词语 Specialized Vocabulary

1.	硬件	yìngjiàn	n.	hardware
2.	软件	ruǎnjiàn	n.	software
3.	安装包	ānzhuāngbāo	n.	installation package
4.	扫描	sǎomiáo	v.	scan
5.	二维码	èrwéimǎ	n.	QR code
6.	下载	xiàzài	v.	download

cíyǔ
词语
Vocabulary

7.	智慧生活	zhìhuì shēnghuó	phr.	AI Life
	智慧	zhìhuì	n.	wisdom, intelligence
	生活	shēnghuó	n.	life

补充专业词语 Supplementary Specialized Vocabulary

1.	搜索	sōusuǒ	v.	search
2.	穿墙性	chuānqiángxìng	n.	penetrability
3.	覆盖区域	fùgài qūyù	phr.	coverage area
4.	密码	mìmǎ	n.	password

jùzi
句子
Sentences

1. 请问今天有什么安排？
2. 看得见、摸得着的是硬件。
3. 手机里面安装的安装包是软件。
4. 安装硬件要连接网线和电源。
5. 安装软件要扫描二维码，下载并安装。

7

Jìsuànjī shàngwǎng shèzhì

计算机上网设置

Setting the Computer Internet Access

jìsuànjī wúxiàn shàngwǎng de pèizhì bùzhòu

计算机无线上网的配置步骤

Steps of Configuring the Wi-Fi

diǎnjī píngmù yòu-xiàfāng de "diànnǎo" huò

点击屏幕右下方的"电脑"或

"wúxiànwǎng" túbiāo

"无线网"图标

click the "computer" or "wireless network" icon at the bottom right of the screen

diǎnjī wúxiànwǎng míngchēng

点击无线网名称

click the desired wireless network

diǎnjī "zìdòng liánjiē"

点击"自动连接"

click "Auto Connect"

diǎnjī "liánjiē"

点击"连接"

click "connect"

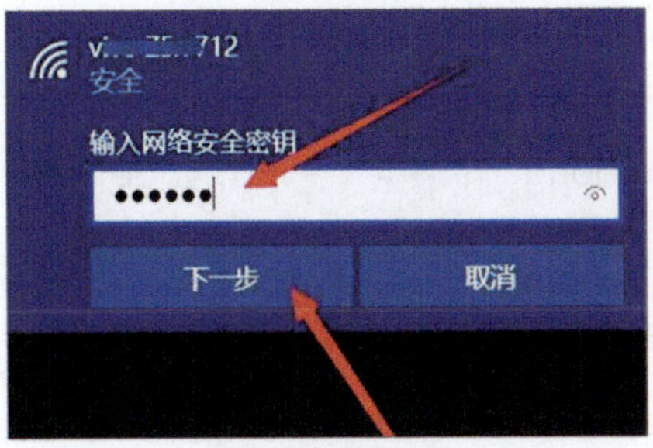

shūrù mìyào

输入密钥

enter the encryption key

题解 Introduction

1. 学习内容：计算机上网的方法和步骤。
   Learning content: The methods and procedures of setting the computer Internet access.
2. 知识目标：掌握 ü 或者以 ü 开头的韵母跟 j、q、x 相拼时的拼写规则和“一”的变调，掌握与计算机上网设置相关的核心词语与表达。
   Knowledge target: Learn the spelling rules of “ü” or finals beginning with “ü” combined it spells with “j”, “q” and “x” and the tone sandhi of “一”; master the keywords and expressions related to the setting of computer Internet access.
3. 技能目标：能够对计算机上网进行设置。
   Skill target: Be able to set the computer Internet access.

第一部分 Part 1

语音 *Phonetic Learning*

一、语音知识 yǔyīn zhīshi Knowledge about Phonetics

1. 拼写规则（3） Spelling rules (3)

ü 或者以 ü 开头的韵母跟 j、q、x 相拼的时候，省略 ü 上边的两点，写成 ju、qu、xu、jue、que、xue、juan、quan、xuan、jun、qun、xun。跟 n、l 相拼的时候，ü 上边的两点不能省略，写成 nü、lü、lüe、nüe。

When “ü” or a final beginning with “ü” is combined with “j”, “q” or “x”, “ü” is written as “u” like in “ju”, “qu”, “xu”, “jue”, “que”, “xue”, “juan”, “quan”, “xuan”, “jun”, “qun”, “xun”. When combined with “n” or “l”, the two dots above “ü” can not be removed. For example, “nü”, “lü”, “lüe”, “nüe”.

2. “一”的变调 Tone sandhi of “一”

数词“一”本调是第一声。“一”后边的音节是第一声、第二声、第三声时，“一”读作“yì”；“一”后边的音节是第四声时，“一”读作“yí”。例如：

The numeral “一” is pronounced as “yī” when it stands by itself. “一” is pronounced as “yì” when it precedes a first-tone, second-tone or third-tone syllable. It is read as “yí” when it precedes a fourth-tone syllable. For example,

一斤 yì jīn　　一台 yì tái　　一种 yì zhǒng　　一个 yí gè

二、语音练习 yǔyīn liànxí Phonetic Exercises

读一读 Let’s read.

① 计算机 jìsuànjī　② 上网 shàngwǎng　③ 子网 zǐwǎng　④ 掩码 yǎnmǎ

⑤ mòrèn 默认	⑥ wǎngguān 网关	⑦ xìnxī 信息	⑧ diàoxiàn 掉线
⑨ wěndìngxìng 稳定性	⑩ kànggānrǎoxìng 抗干扰性	⑪ dēnglù 登录	⑫ zìdòng 自动

第二部分 Part 2

课文 Texts

一、热身 rèshēn Warm-up

1. 下面是计算机上网设置的几种方法，请仔细查看有什么不同，并选出你觉得可能是最简单的一种。

Here are several ways to set the computer Internet access. Carefully find the differences and choose the simplest one in your opinion.

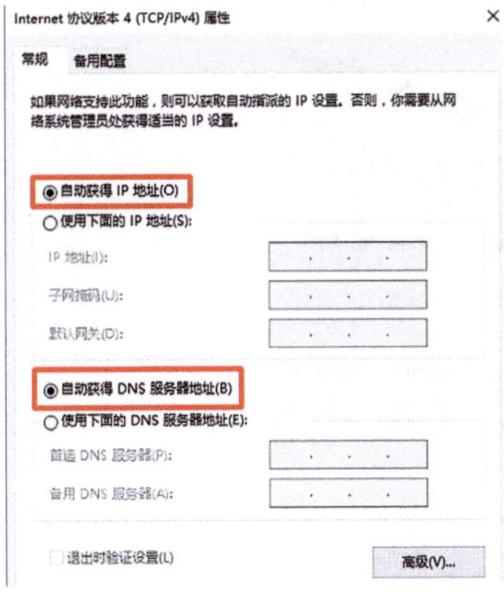

A.

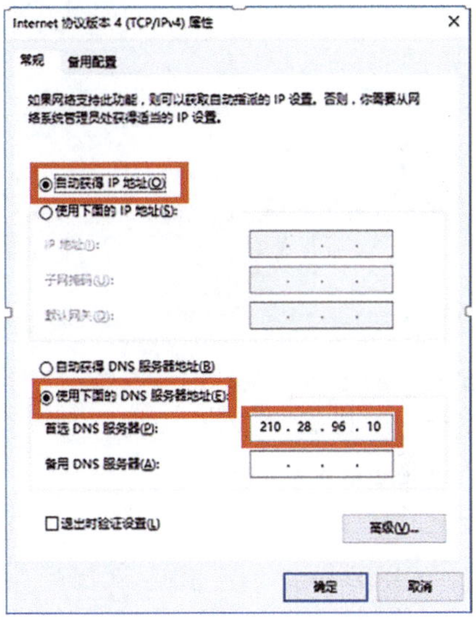

B.

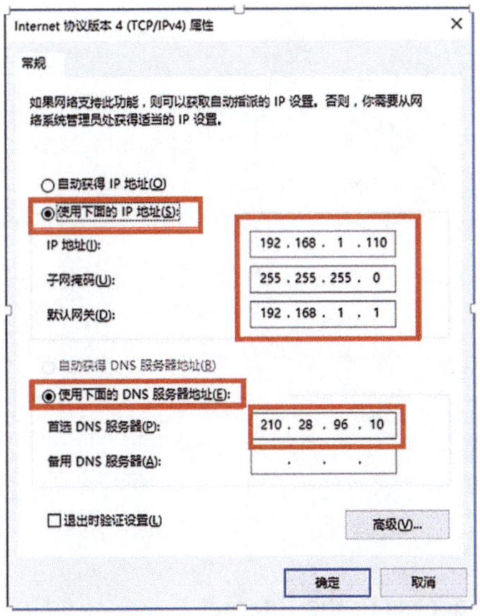

C.

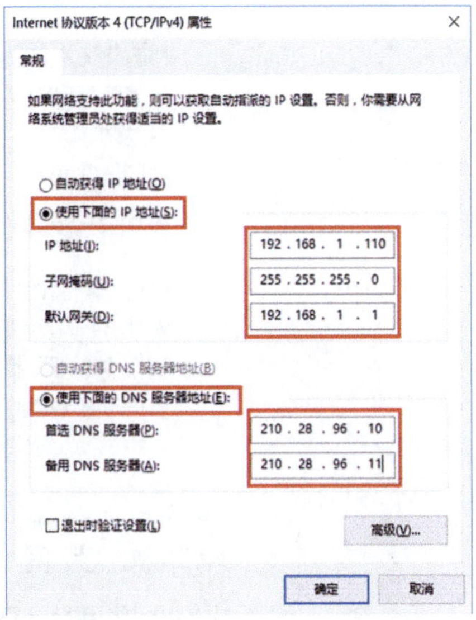

D.

Yǐshàng jìsuànjī shàngwǎng shèzhì de fāngfǎ zhōng, nǐ rènwéi zuì jiǎndān de yì zhǒng kěnéng shì:
以上计算机上网设置的方法中，你认为最简单的一种可能是：________。
Of the above ways to set the computer Internet access, the simplest one in your opinion is:

2. 观看介绍 IP 地址的视频，并选出正确答案。

Watch the video about the IP address and choose the correct answer.

shì yí gè diànhuà hàomǎ
A. 是一个电话号码
It's a telephone number.

shì yí gè yóuzhèng biānmǎ
B. 是一个邮政编码
It's a postal code.

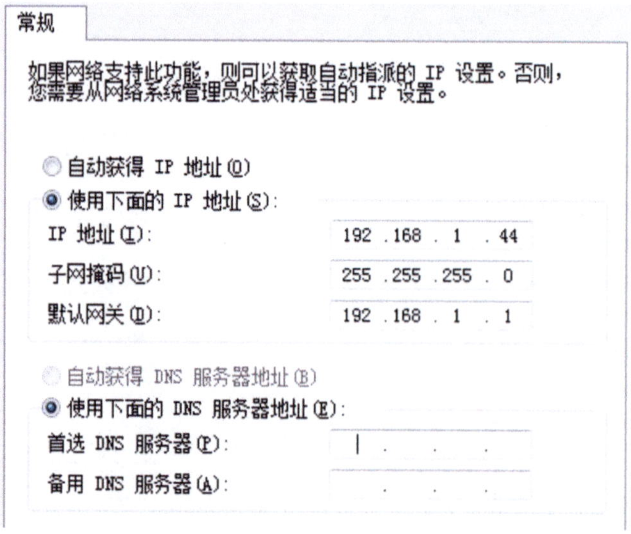

jìsuànjī shàngwǎng xūyào de dìzhǐ
C. 计算机上网需要的地址
It's an address a computer needs to get access to the Internet.

Guānyú IP dìzhǐ, zhèngquè de shuōfǎ shì:
关于 IP 地址，正确的说法是：________。
The correct statement about the IP address is:

二、课文 kèwén Texts

A 07-01

túdì: Shīfu, jīntiān tiānqì zěnmeyàng?
徒弟：师傅，今天天气怎么样？

shīfu: Jīntiān tiānqì hěn hǎo, bù lěng yě bú rè.
师傅：今天天气很好，不冷也不热。

túdì: Wǒ xiǎng zhīdào, jìsuànjī yào shàngwǎng, yīnggāi zěnme bàn?
徒弟：我想知道，计算机要上网，应该怎么办？

shīfu: Shǒuxiān yào zhèngquè liánjiē wǎngxiàn.
师傅：首先要正确连接网线。

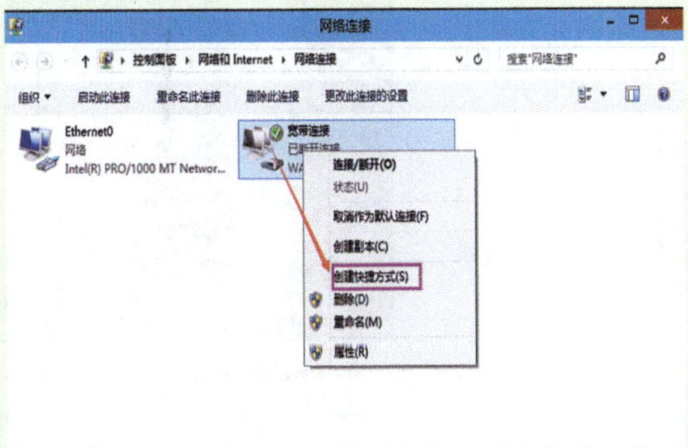

译文 yìwén Text in English

Apprentice: Master, what's the weather like today?
Master: It's a fine day today. It's neither cold nor hot.
Apprentice: I wonder what I should do if I want the computer to get access to the Internet.
Master: First, connect the network cable correctly.

普通词语 pǔtōng cíyǔ General Vocabulary

07-02

1.	天气	tiānqì	n.	weather
2.	怎么样	zěnmeyàng	pron.	what about
3.	不	bù	adv.	not, no
4.	冷	lěng	adj.	cold
5.	也	yě	adv.	also
6.	热	rè	adj.	hot
7.	想	xiǎng	aux.	want
8.	应该	yīnggāi	aux.	ought to
9.	怎么办	zěnme bàn	phr.	what to do
	怎么	zěnme	pron.	what about, in what way
10.	首先	shǒuxiān	adv.	first of all
11.	正确	zhèngquè	adj.	correct

专业词语 zhuānyè cíyǔ Specialized Vocabulary

07-03

1.	计算机	jìsuànjī	n.	computer
2.	上网	shàng//wǎng	v.	get access to the Internet

B 07-04

túdì: Shīfu, zhèngquè liánjiē wǎngxiàn yǐhòu, jiù néng shàngwǎng le ma?
徒弟：师傅，正确 连接 网线 以后，就 能 上网 了吗？

shīfu: Bú shì de, yào shèzhì jìsuànjī de IP dìzhǐ、zǐwǎng yǎnmǎ、mòrèn wǎngguān、DNS fúwùqì dìzhǐ.
师傅：不是的，要设置计算机的 IP 地址、子网 掩码、默认 网关、DNS 服务器地址。

túdì: Rúhé dédào zhèxiē xìnxī ne?
徒弟：如何得到这些信息呢？

shīfu: Yóu wǎngluò guǎnlǐyuán tígōng.
师傅：由 网络 管理员提供。

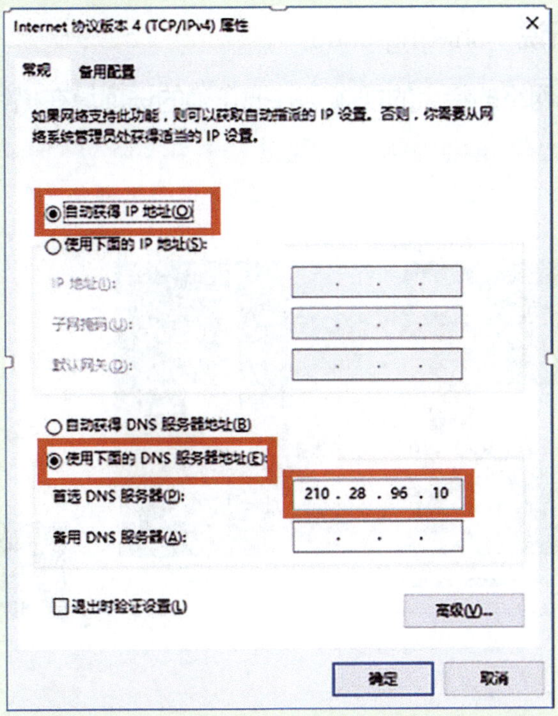

译文 yìwén Text in English

Apprentice: Master, can I surf the Internet after connecting the cable correctly?

Master: No, you should set the IP address, subnet mask, default gateway and DNS server address of the computer.

Apprentice: How do I get the information?

Master: It is provided by the network administrator.

普通词语 pǔtōng cíyǔ General Vocabulary

07-05

1.	以后	yǐhòu	n.	subsequence
2.	了	le	part.	*an aspect particle indicating a change of state*
3.	得到	dé//dào	v.	get, obtain
4.	管理员	guǎnlǐyuán	n.	administrator
5.	提供	tígōng	v.	provide

专业词语 zhuānyè cíyǔ Specialized Vocabulary

07-06

1.	子网掩码	zǐwǎng yǎnmǎ	phr.	subnet mask
	子网	zǐwǎng	n.	subnet
	掩码	yǎnmǎ	n.	mask

2.	默认网关	mòrèn wǎngguān	phr.	default gateway
3.	信息	xìnxī	n.	information

三、视听说 shì-tīng-shuō Viewing, Listening & Speaking

1. 观看介绍有线网络和无线网络的特点的视频，并把正确的选项填在横线上。

Watch the video about the characteristics of wired and wireless networks, and fill in the blanks with correct answers.

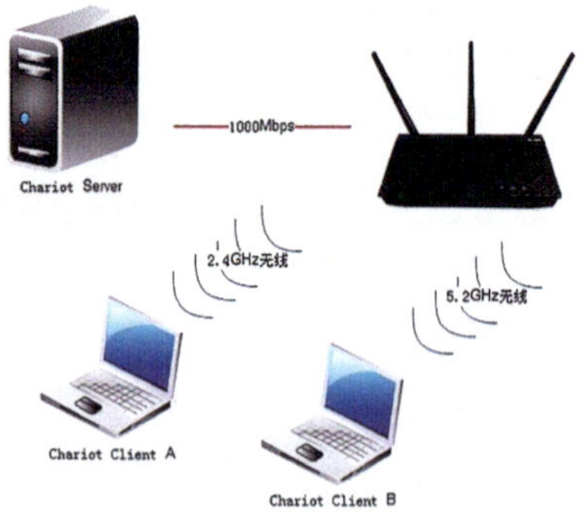

bù xūyào wǎngxiàn
A. 不需要 网线
no network cable required

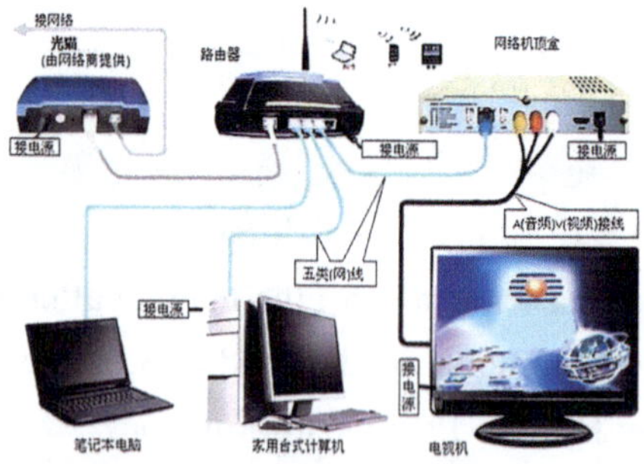

zài gùdìngdiǎn shǐyòng
B. 在固定点 使用
used at fixed sites

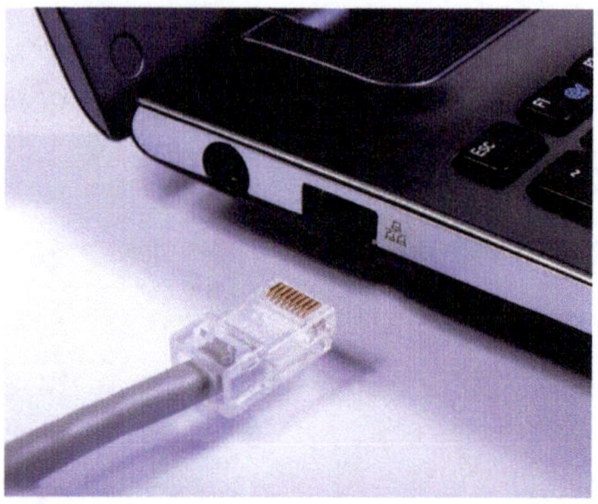

xūyào wǎngxiàn
C. 需要 网线
network cable needed

zài yídìng fànwéi nèi línghuó shǐyòng
D. 在一定范围内灵活 使用
used flexibly within a certain range

huì chūxiàn diàoxiàn xiànxiàng
E. 会 出现 掉线 现象
occasionally disconnected

wěndìng
F. 稳定
stable

Yǒuxiàn wǎngluò de tèdiǎn shì:
① 有线 网络的特点是：______________。
Characteristics of the wired network are:

Wúxiàn wǎngluò de tèdiǎn shì:
② 无线 网络的特点是：______________。
Characteristics of the wireless network are:

2. 说一说 Let's talk.

请说出有线网络和无线网络的主要特点和优势。

Please speak out the main features and advantages of wired and wireless networks.

四、学以致用 xuéyǐzhìyòng Practicing What You Have Learnt

观看介绍计算机使用无线网络上网的视频，并选出正确答案。

Watch the video about using the computer to surf the Internet through Wi-Fi, and choose the correct answers.

bǎohù diànnǎo zhōng de zhòngyào xìnxī
A. 保护电脑中的重要信息
To protect the important information in the computer.

fǒuzé diànnǎo huì chū wèntí
B. 否则电脑会出问题
The computer will otherwise go wrong.

yīnwèi diànnǎo tài lèi le
C. 因为电脑太累了
The computer is too tired.

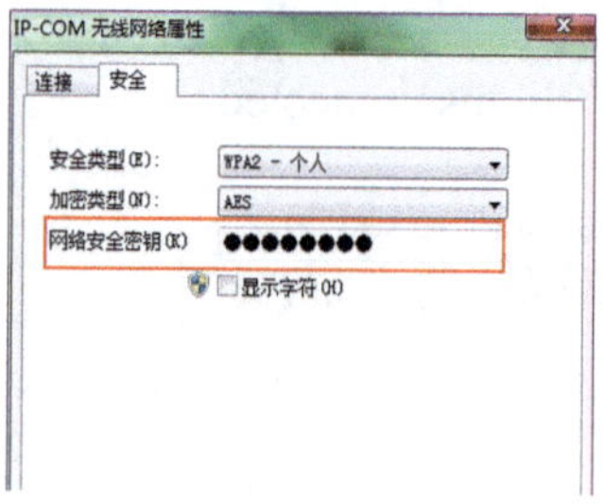

yòng mìmǎ dēnglù cái ānquán
D. 用密码登录才安全
It's safer to log in with a password.

Wèi shénme yào guāndiào zìdòng liánjiē?
为什么要关掉自动连接？
Why should the auto connection be turned off?

Yīnwèi:
因为：__________。
Because:

补充专业词语 bǔchōng zhuānyè cíyǔ Supplementary Specialized Vocabulary

07-07

1.	掉线	diào//xiàn	v.	disconnect
2.	稳定性	wěndìngxìng	n.	stability
3.	抗干扰性	kànggānrǎoxìng	n.	interference immunity
4.	登录	dēnglù	v.	log in/onto
5.	自动连接	zìdòng liánjiē	phr.	auto connection
6.	密钥	mìyào	n.	encryption key

第三部分 Part 3

课堂用语 Classroom Expressions

1. 最近学习怎么样？ Zuìjìn xuéxí zěnmeyàng? How about your studies these days?
2. 你有事吗？ Nǐ yǒu shì ma? Can I help you?/What's up?

第四部分 Part 4

单元实训 Unit Practical Training

获取动态 IP 地址 huòqǔ dòngtài IP dìzhǐ Obtaining a Dynamic IP Address

实训目的 Training purpose

掌握计算机使用有线网络上网的方法。

Master the method of surfing the Internet on the computer via a wired network.

实训内容 Training content

计算机通过有线网络连接上网。

Connecting the computer to the Internet via a wired network.

实训组织 Training organization

每 3 ～ 4 人一组，选出小组长。

Students work in groups of 3-4. Each group chooses a group leader.

实训步骤 Training steps

1. 将路由器的 WAN 口接入互联网，并用网线把交换机端口接入路由器的 LAN 口。
   Connect the WAN port of the router to the Internet, and connect the switch port to the LAN port of the router with the network cable.
2. 用网线把计算机的 RJ45 口接到交换机端口，观察路由器的灯是否亮，交换机的灯是否亮，并观察计算机网卡的灯是否亮。
   Connect the RJ45 port of the computer to the switch port with the network cable, and observe whether the router lights are on, whether the switch indicator light is on, and whether the computer's network interface card indicator light is on.
3. 设置自动获得IP地址、自动获得DNS服务器地址。
   Set the "Obtaining IP Address Automatically" and the "Obtaining DNS Server Address Automatically".

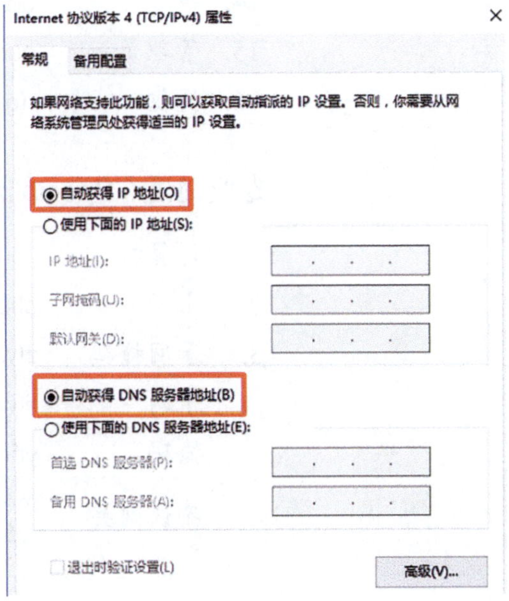

④ 打开浏览器，输入一个网址，看是否能上网。

Open the browser and enter a Uniform Resource Locator (URL) to see if you can surf the Internet.

⑤ 学员总结，教师总评。

The students make a summary and the teacher comments on the training.

第五部分 Part 5

单元小结 Unit Summary

cíyǔ
词语
Vocabulary

普通词语 General Vocabulary

1.	天气	tiānqì	n.	weather
2.	怎么样	zěnmeyàng	pron.	what about
3.	不	bù	adv.	not, no
4.	冷	lěng	adj.	cold
5.	也	yě	adv.	also
6.	热	rè	adj.	hot
7.	想	xiǎng	aux.	want
8.	应该	yīnggāi	aux.	ought to
9.	怎么办	zěnme bàn	phr.	what to do
	怎么	zěnme	pron.	what about, in what way
10.	首先	shǒuxiān	adv.	first of all
11.	正确	zhèngquè	adj.	correct
12.	以后	yǐhòu	n.	subsequence
13.	了	le	part.	*an aspect particle indicating a change of state*
14.	得到	dé//dào	v.	get, obtain
15.	管理员	guǎnlǐyuán	n.	administrator
16.	提供	tígōng	v.	provide

专业词语 Specialized Vocabulary

1.	计算机	jìsuànjī	n.	computer
2.	上网	shàng//wǎng	v.	get access to the Internet
3.	子网掩码	zǐwǎng yǎnmǎ	phr.	subnet mask
	子网	zǐwǎng	n.	subnet
	掩码	yǎnmǎ	n.	mask
4.	默认网关	mòrèn wǎngguān	phr.	default gateway

cíyǔ
词语
Vocabulary

5.	信息	xìnxī	n.	information

补充专业词语 Supplementary Specialized Vocabulary

1.	掉线	diào//xiàn	v.	disconnect
2.	稳定性	wěndìngxìng	n.	stability
3.	抗干扰性	kànggānrǎoxìng	n.	interference immunity
4.	登录	dēnglù	v.	log in/onto
5.	自动连接	zìdòng liánjiē	phr.	auto connection
6.	密钥	mìyào	n.	encryption key

jùzi
句子
Sentences

1. 今天天气很好，不冷也不热。
2. 正确连接网线以后，就能上网了吗？
3. 要设置计算机的 IP 地址、子网掩码、默认网关、DNS 服务器地址，这些信息由网络管理员提供。

8

Wǎngluò cèshì

网络测试

Network Testing

jìsuànjī shàngwǎng cèshì

计算机 上网 测试

Testing the Internet Access of the Computer

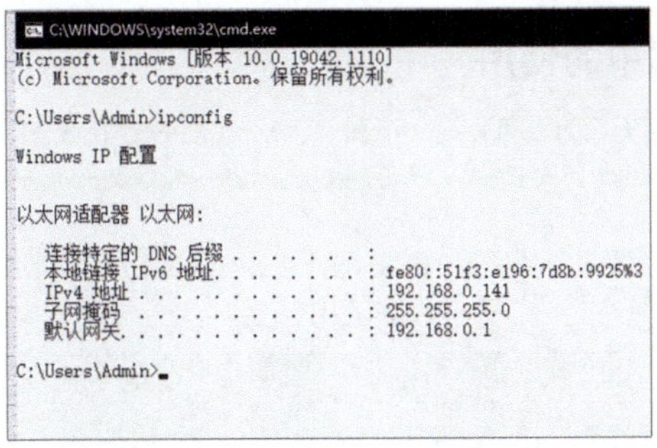

shǐyòng ipconfig mìnglìng, dedào jìsuànjī de

使用 ipconfig 命令，得到计算机的

IP dìzhǐ、 mòrèn wǎngguān dìzhǐ

IP 地址、默认 网关 地址

use the ipconfig command to get the computer's IP address and default gateway address

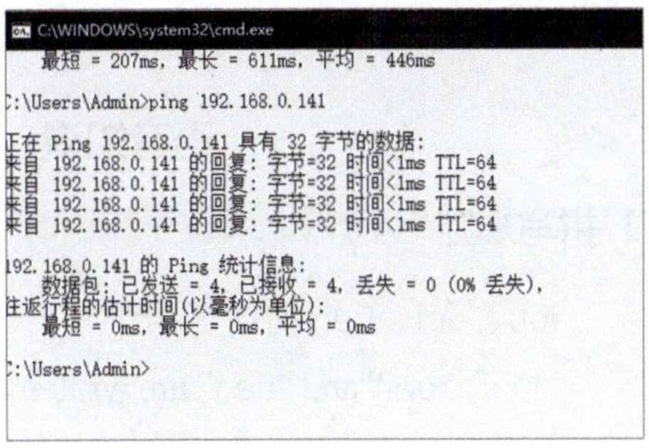

shǐyòng ping mìnglìng,

使用 ping 命令，

ping jìsuànjī zìjǐ de IP dìzhǐ

ping 计算机自己的 IP 地址

use the ping command to ping the computer's own IP address

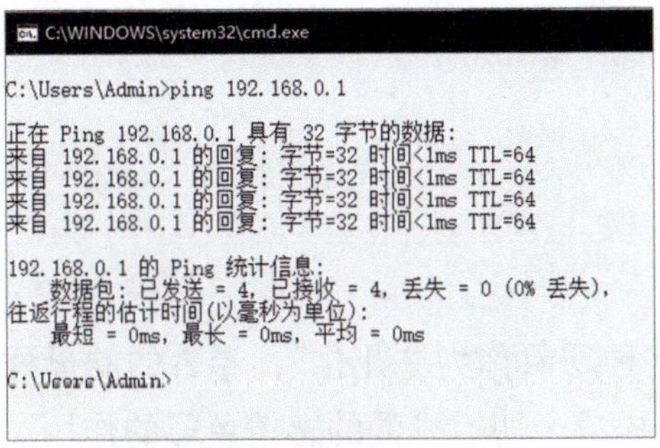

shǐyòng ping mìnglìng,

使用 ping 命令，

ping mòrèn wǎngguān dìzhǐ

ping 默认 网关 地址

use the ping command to ping the default gateway address

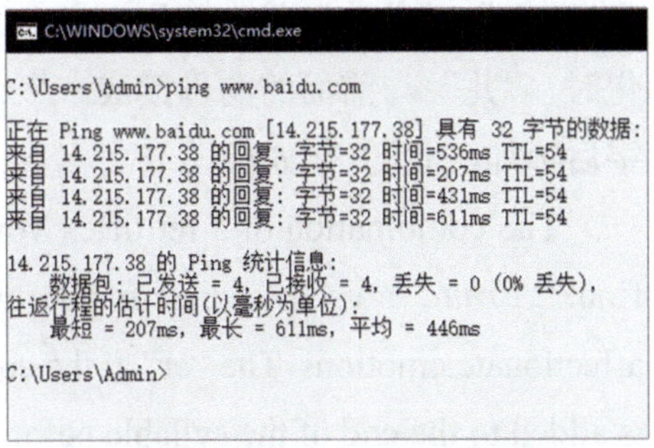

ping mǒu yí gè wǎngzhǐ

ping 某一个网址

ping a certain website address

题解 Introduction

1. 学习内容：ipconfig/all 命令、ping 命令和带参数 -t 的 ping 命令等在网络测试中的使用及具体操作。
   Learning content: The use and operation of the ipconfig/all command, ping command and ping command with the parameter -t in network testing.
2. 知识目标：掌握 iou、uei、uen 前面有声母时的拼写规则、儿化的基本知识，掌握与网络测试相关的核心词语及表达。
   Knowledge target: Master the spelling rules when "iou", "uei" and "uen" are preceded by initials and the basic knowledge of *erhua*; master the key words and expressions related to network testing.
3. 技能目标：掌握 ipconfig 和 ping 命令在网络连通测试中的使用。
   Skill target: Master the use of the ipconfig and ping commands in the network access testing.

第一部分 Part 1

语音 Phonetic Learning

一、语音知识 yǔyīn zhīshi Knowledge about Phonetics

1. 拼写规则（4） Spelling rules (4)

iou、uei、uen 前面有声母时，写成 iu、ui、un。例如：

"iou", "uei" and "uen" are written as "iu", "ui" and "un" after initials. For example,

n + iou → n + iu → niu

g + uei → g + ui → gui

l + uen → l + un → lun

2. 儿化 *Erhua*

卷舌元音 er 与其他韵母结合，使韵母带上卷舌色彩，这种现象称为"儿化"，卷舌的韵母称为"儿化韵"。"儿化"具有区别词义、区分词性和表示细小、轻松或亲切、喜爱的感情色彩的作用。儿化时，"儿"与前面的韵母读成一个音节。拼写时在前面韵母末尾加上"r"，汉字写法是在原来的汉字后边加"儿"。例如：

The combination of a retroflex vowel "er" with a final is called "*erhua*", and the final is called "*erhua* final". *Erhua* is used to discriminate word meanings and parts of speech, and express subtle, relaxed, or affectionate emotions. The "*er*" at the end is pronounced together with the syllable before it. In spelling, an "r" is added to the end of the syllable before it, and "儿" is added to the end of the original Chinese character. For example,

nǎ + er → nǎr（哪儿）

zhè + er → zhèr（这儿）

二、语音练习 yǔyīn liànxí Phonetic Exercises

读一读 Let's read.

① cèshì 测试	② mìnglìng 命令	③ tíshìfú 提示符	④ shūrù 输入
⑤ ping mìnglìng ping 命令	⑥ liántōngxìng 连通性	⑦ liánwǎng 联网	⑧ cānshù 参数
⑨ yùnxíng 运行	⑩ wǎngsù 网速	⑪ hǎo de 好的	⑫ zài 在

第二部分 Part 2

课文 Texts

一、热身 rèshēn Warm-up

1. 给词语选择对应的图片。Match the pictures with corresponding words.

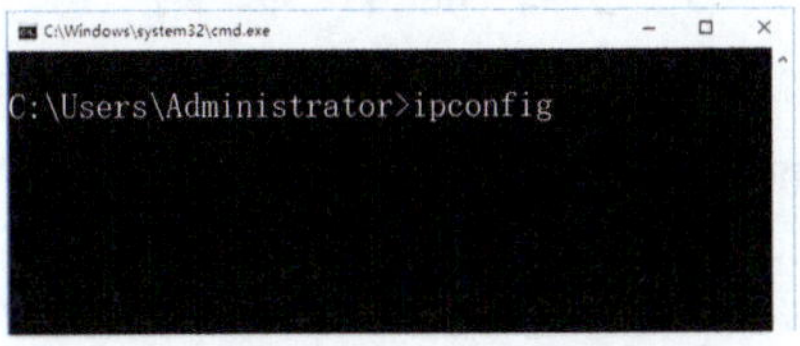

A.

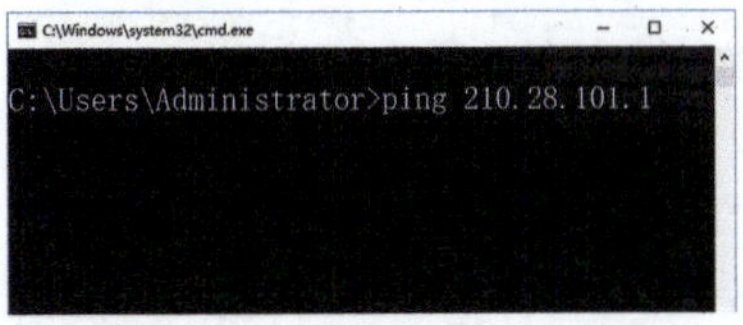

B.

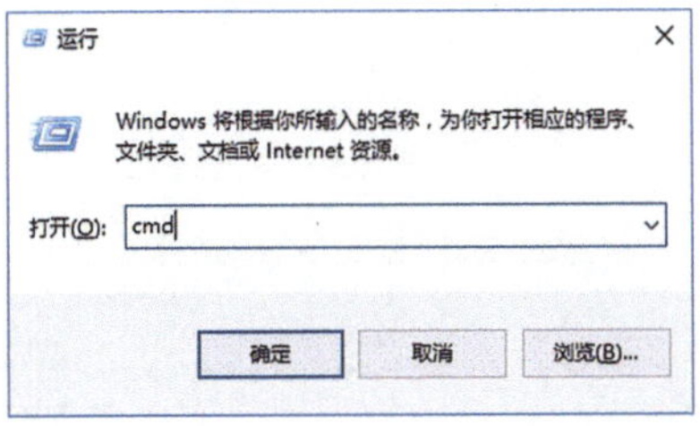

C.

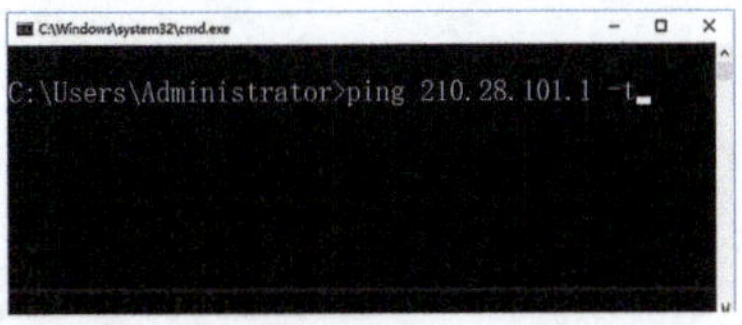

D.

① yùnxíng mìnglìng 运行命令 ______ running command

② ipconfig mìnglìng ipconfig 命令 ______ ipconfig command

③ ping mìnglìng ping 命令 ______ ping command

④ dài cānshù ping mìnglìng 带参数 ping 命令 ______ ping command with parameters

2. 观看介绍网络测试的视频，并将下面任务中属于网络测试的工作填在横线上。

Watch the video about network testing, and fill in the blanks with the jobs that fall under the category of network testing among the following tasks.

cèshì wǎngsù
A. 测试网速
testing the network speed

cèshì diànnǎo néngfǒu shàngwǎng
B. 测试电脑能否上网
checking whether the computer can access the Internet

chákàn diànnǎo jiàgé
C. 查看电脑价格
checking the price of the computer

chákàn liǎng tái diànnǎo néngfǒu liánwǎng
D. 查看两台电脑能否联网
checking whether the two computers are connected through the Internet

chákàn zhǔjī de jìsuànjī míng
E. 查看主机的计算机名
checking the computer name of the host

chákàn zhǔjī de IP dìzhǐ
F. 查看主机的 IP 地址
checking the IP address of the host

Wǎngluò cèshì de zhǔyào gōngzuò bāokuò:
网络测试的主要工作包括：____________。
The main jobs of network testing include:

二、课文 kèwén Texts

A 08-01

shīfu: Jīntiān xuéxí wǎngluò cèshì. Nǐ zài mìnglìng tíshìfú hòu shūrù “ipconfig/all”.
师傅：今天学习网络测试。你在命令提示符后输入“ipconfig/all”。

túdì: Hǎo de, wǒ zhèngzài shūrù. Zhège mìnglìng yǒu shénme yòng?
徒弟：好的，我正在输入。这个命令有什么用？

shīfu: Kěyǐ yòng tā lái chákàn zhǔjī de IP dìzhǐ.
师傅：可以用它来查看主机的IP地址。

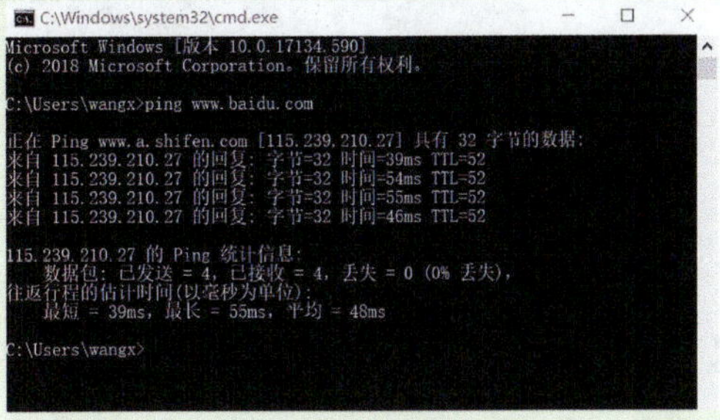

译文 yìwén Text in English

Master: Today we’re going to learn the network testing. Enter “ipconfig/all” in the command prompt.
Apprentice: OK, I’m entering the command. What’s this command used for?
Master: It can be used to view the IP address of the host.

普通词语 pǔtōng cíyǔ General Vocabulary

08-02

1.	在	zài	prep.	in
2.	后	hòu	n.	back
3.	好的	hǎo de	phr.	OK, all right
4.	正在	zhèngzài	adv.	just
5.	这个	zhège	pron.	this
6.	用	yòng	n.	use
7.	可以	kěyǐ	aux.	may, can
8.	它	tā	pron.	it
9.	来	lái	v.	be here
10.	查看	chákàn	v.	view, examine, check

专业词语 zhuānyè cíyǔ Specialized Vocabulary

08-03

1.	测试	cèshì	n.	test
2.	命令	mìnglìng	n.	command
3.	提示符	tíshìfú	n.	prompt
4.	输入	shūrù	v.	type in

B 08-04

túdì: Ping mìnglìng kěyǐ chákàn diànnǎo de IP dìzhǐ ma?
徒弟：Ping 命令可以查看电脑的 IP 地址吗？

shīfu: Bù kěyǐ. Tā kěyǐ cèshì diànnǎo néngfǒu shàngwǎng hé liǎng tái diànnǎo de liántōngxìng.
师傅：不可以。它可以测试电脑能否上网和两台电脑的连通性。

túdì: Rúguǒ xūyào guānchá diànnǎo shìfǒu yìzhí liánwǎng, yòng shénme mìnglìng?
徒弟：如果需要观察电脑是否一直联网，用什么命令？

shīfu: Dài cānshù -t ping mìnglìng.
师傅：带参数 -t ping 命令。

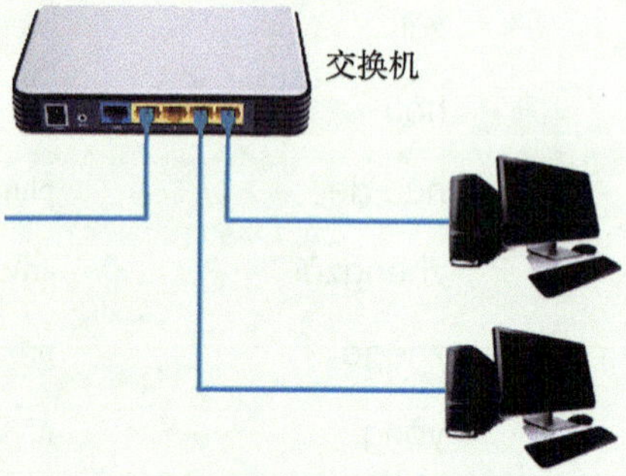

译文 yìwén Text in English

Apprentice: Can the ping command be used to view the IP address of the computer?

Master: No. It can be used to test whether the computer can get access to the Internet and the connectivity of two computers.

Apprentice: If I want to observe whether the computer has been connected to the Internet, what command should I use?

Master: You need to use the ping command with the parameter -t.

普通词语 pǔtōng cíyǔ General Vocabulary

08-05

1.	能否	néngfǒu	v.	can or cannot
2.	两	liǎng	num.	two
3.	台	tái	m.	*a measure word for certain devices*
4.	如果	rúguǒ	conj.	if
5.	观察	guānchá	v.	observe
6.	是否	shìfǒu	adv.	yes or no
7.	一直	yìzhí	adv.	all the time
8.	带	dài	v.	carry with, be accompanied by

专业词语 zhuānyè cíyǔ Specialized Vocabulary

08-06

1.	ping 命令	ping mìnglìng	phr.	ping command
2.	联网	lián//wǎng	v.	be connected to the Internet
3.	参数	cānshù	n.	parameter

三、视听说 shì-tīng-shuō Viewing, Listening & Speaking

1. 观看测试计算机能否上网的视频，根据流程，将下列具体操作步骤排序。

Watch the video about testing whether the computer can get access to the Internet, and put the following specific operation steps in correct order according to the procedure.

Shǐyòng ipconfig mìnglìng, dédào jìsuànjī de IP dìzhǐ、 mòrèn wǎngguān dìzhǐ.
A. 使用 ipconfig 命令，得到计算机的 IP 地址、默认 网关 地址。
Use the ipconfig command to get the computer's IP address and default gateway address.

Shǐyòng ping mìnglìng, ping mòrèn wǎngguān dìzhǐ.
B. 使用 ping 命令，ping 默认 网关 地址。
Use the ping command to ping the default gateway address.

Ping mǒu yí gè wǎngzhǐ.
C. Ping 某一个网址。
Ping a certain address.

Shǐyòng ping mìnglìng, ping jìsuànjī zìjǐ de IP dìzhǐ.
D. 使用 ping 命令，ping 计算机自己的 IP 地址。
Use the ping command to ping the computer's own IP address.

2. 说一说 Let's talk.

请说出测试计算机能否上网的步骤。

Please speak out the steps of testing whether the computer can get access to the Internet.

四、学以致用 xuéyǐzhìyòng Practicing What You Have Learnt

观看介绍网络测试几种命令的用途视频，将命令与各自的用途连线。

Watch the video about the uses of several commands for network testing, and match the commands with their uses respectively.

yùnxíng mìnglìng
① 运行 命令
running command

ipconfig mìnglìng
② ipconfig 命令
ipconfig command

ping mìnglìng
③ ping 命令
ping command

dàicānshù -t ping mìnglìng
④ 带参数 -t ping 命令
ping command with the parameter -t

chákàn zhǔjī de IP dìzhǐ
A. 查看主机的 IP 地址
to view the IP address of the host

dǎkāi mìnglìng chéngxù jièmiàn
B. 打开命令程序界面
to open the command program interface

chákàn diànnǎo shìfǒu liánwǎng
C. 查看电脑是否联网
to check whether the computer is connected to the Internet

cèshì wǎngsù
D. 测试网速
to test the network speed

cèshì wǎngluò wěndìngxìng
E. 测试网络稳定性
to test the network stability

补充专业词语 bǔchōng zhuānyè cíyǔ Supplementary Specialized Vocabulary

08-07

1.	运行命令	yùnxíng mìnglìng	phr.	running command
2.	网速	wǎngsù	n.	network speed

第三部分 Part 3

课堂用语 Classroom Expressions

1. 请问，图书馆在哪儿？ Qǐngwèn, túshūguǎn zài nǎr? Excuse me, where's the library?
2. 请问，这个汉语怎么说？ Qǐngwèn, zhège Hànyǔ zěnme shuō? Excuse me, how to say it in Chinese?

第四部分 Part 4

单元实训 Unit Practical Training

使用网络测试命令 shǐyòng wǎngluò cèshì mìnglìng Using Network-Testing Commands

实训目的 Training purpose

掌握网络测试命令的使用，培养团队合作精神、竞争意识。

Master the use of network-testing commands, and cultivate the spirit of teamwork and awareness of competition.

实训组织 Training organization

每组 3～5 人。选出一个组长。

Students work in groups of 3-5. Each group chooses a group leader.

实训内容 Training content

ipconfig 和 ping 命令的使用。

The use of the ipconfig and ping commands.

实训步骤 Training steps

1. 将参加实训的人员分成若干小组，每组 3～5 人。轮流上机操作与实践。训练每位同学对知识掌握的程度及操作的熟练程度。具体步骤为：

1）在计算机 PC1 上运行 cmd 命令；

2）输入“ping 210.28.101.100”；

3）当出现下图所示内容：“来自 210.28.101.100 的回复：字节 =32 时间 <1ms TTL=128”，表示 PC1 和 PC2 是联网的。

Divide the students into groups of 3-5. The group members take turns to operate the computer so as to check how well they've mastered the knowledge and how proficiently they operate. The specific steps are as follows:

1) Run the cmd command on the computer PC1;

2) Enter "ping 210.28.101.100";

3) When the following figure appears—the response from 210.28.101.100: byte=32 time<1ms TTL=128, it indicates PC1 and PC2 are connected to the Internet.

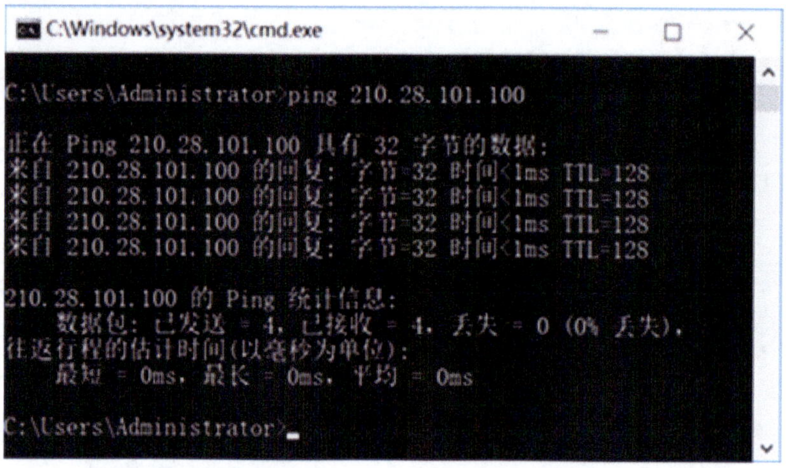

❷ 宣布比赛规则及要求：每组每人可以多次上机操作，安排专人记录每位同学操作所花费的时间，其他组同学监督。

Announce the competition rules and requirements: Each member in each group can operate the computer for multiple times. A person who is specially assigned is responsible for recording the time each group member takes to operate the computer, and the members of other groups supervise the whole process.

❸ 开始比赛。

Start the competition.

❹ 计算每组同学总共花费的时间及得分。

Calculate the time spent and the scores of each group.

❺ 学员总结，教师总评。

The students make a summary and the teacher comments on the training.

第五部分 Part 5

单元小结 Unit Summary

cíyǔ
词语
Vocabulary

普通词语 General Vocabulary

1.	在	zài	prep.	in
2.	后	hòu	n.	back
3.	好的	hǎo de	phr.	OK, all right
4.	正在	zhèngzài	adv.	just
5.	这个	zhège	pron.	this
6.	用	yòng	n.	use
7.	可以	kěyǐ	aux.	may, can
8.	它	tā	pron.	it
9.	来	lái	v.	be here
10.	查看	chákàn	v.	view, examine, check
11.	能否	néngfǒu	v.	can or cannot
12.	两	liǎng	num.	two
13.	台	tái	m.	*a measure word for certain devices*
14.	如果	rúguǒ	conj.	if
15.	观察	guānchá	v.	observe
16.	是否	shìfǒu	adv.	yes or no
17.	一直	yìzhí	adv.	all the time
18.	带	dài	v.	carry with, be accompanied by

专业词语 Specialized Vocabulary

1.	测试	cèshì	n.	test
2.	命令	mìnglìng	n.	command
3.	提示符	tíshìfú	n.	prompt
4.	输入	shūrù	v.	type in
5.	ping 命令	ping mìnglìng	phr.	ping command
6.	联网	lián//wǎng	v.	be connected to the Internet
7.	参数	cānshù	n.	parameter

补充专业词语 Supplementary Specialized Vocabulary

1.	运行命令	yùnxíng mìnglìng	phr.	running command
2.	网速	wǎngsù	n.	network speed

jùzi 句子 Sentences	1. 你在命令提示符后输入“ipconfig/all”。 2. 我正在输入。 3. ipconfig/all 命令可以查看主机的 IP 地址。 4. ping 命令可以测试电脑是否能上网。 5. ping 命令还可以测试两台电脑的连通性。

9 Huìzhì wǎngluò tuòpūtú
绘制网络拓扑图
Drawing a Network Topology Diagram

huìzhì wǎngluò tuòpūtú

绘制 网络 拓扑图

Drawing a Network Topology Diagram

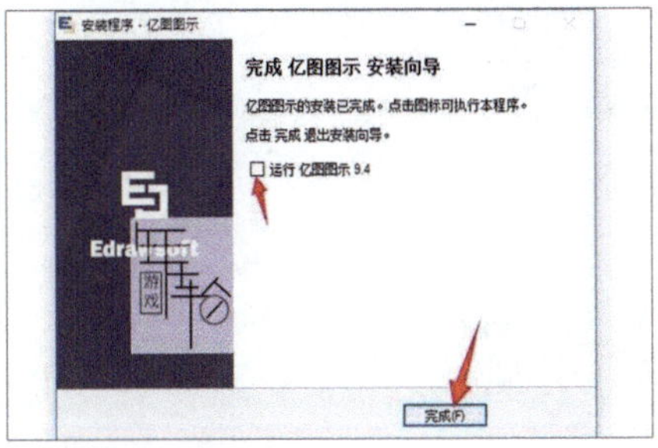

ānzhuāng hǎo “Yìtú Túshì”

安装 好“亿图图示”

install EdrawMax

jiāng shèbèi túbiāo dǎorù fúhàokù

将 设备图标导入符号库

import the device icons into the symbol library

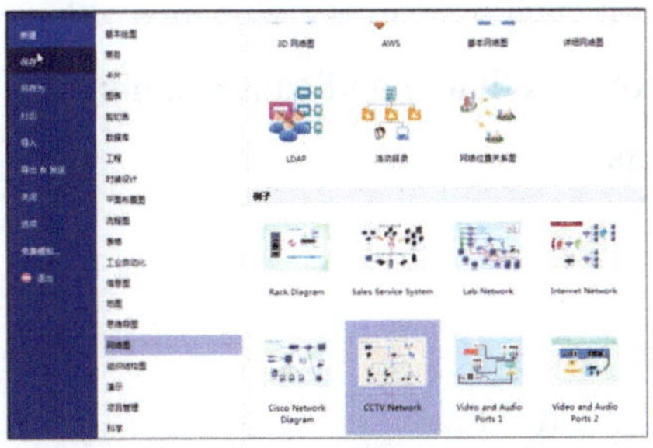

xīn jiàn wǎngluò tuòpū

新建 网络 拓扑

create a new network topology

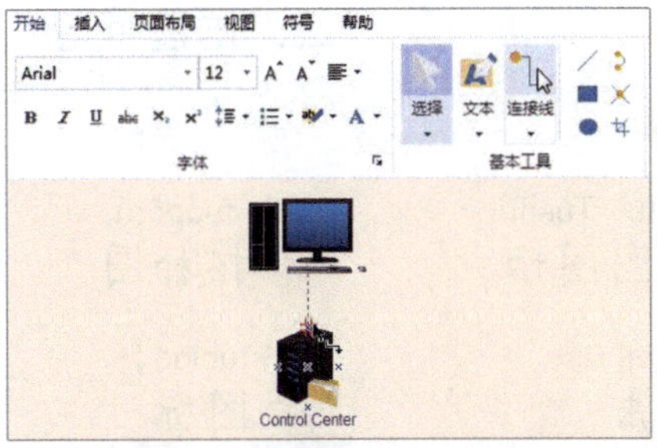

tiānjiā shèbèi， ránhòu

添加设备，然后

zài shèbèi jiān tiānjiā liánjiēxiàn

在设备 间添加连接线

add devices and add connecting lines between the devices

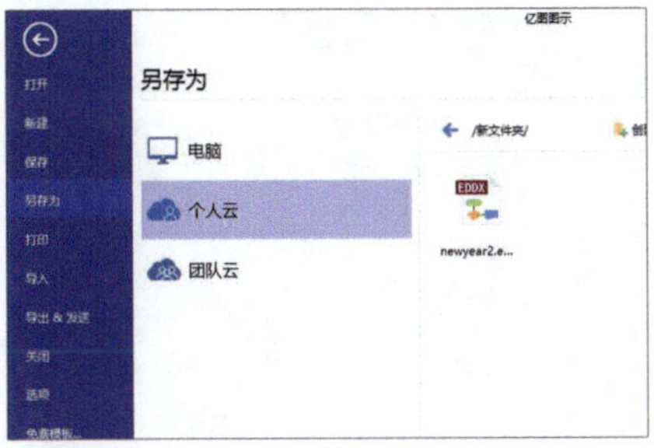

bǎocún tuòpūtú

保存 拓扑图

save the topology diagram

题解 Introduction

1. 学习内容：运用亿图图示软件画网络拓扑图的方法与步骤等。
   Learning content: The methods and process of drawing a network topology diagram with the software EdrawMax.
2. 知识目标：掌握隔音符号的基本知识，掌握与画网络拓扑图相关的核心词语及表达。
   Knowledge target: Master the basic knowledge of the syllable-dividing mark; master the key words and expressions related to drawing network topology diagrams.
3. 技能目标：掌握运用亿图图示软件画网络拓扑图的方法与步骤。
   Skill target: Master the methods and steps of drawing network topology diagrams with the software EdrawMax.

第一部分 Part 1

语音 Phonetic Learning

一、语音知识 yǔyīn zhīshi Knowledge about Phonetics

拼写规则（5）：隔音符号的用法 Spelling rules (5): The usage of the syllable-dividing mark

a、o、e 开头的音节连接在其他音节后边的时候，如果音节的界限发生混淆，要使用隔音符号“ ’ ”隔开。如：

When a syllable beginning with “a”, “o”, or “e” comes after another syllable and causes ambiguity, the syllable-dividing mark “ ’ ” is used to distinguish the syllables. For example,

xī + ān → xiān（先）→ Xi’ān（西安）

pí + ǎo → piǎo（漂）→ pí’ǎo（皮袄）

二、语音练习 yǔyīn liànxí Phonetic Exercises

读一读 Let’s read.

① Yìtú Túshì 亿图图示	② tuòpūtú 拓扑图	③ xuǎnxiàng 选项	④ múbǎn 模板
⑤ diǎnjī 点击	⑥ túbiāo 图标	⑦ liánjiēxiàn 连接线	⑧ xuǎnsèqū 选色区
⑨ bǎocún 保存	⑩ dǎochū 导出	⑪ géshì 格式	⑫ wénběn 文本

第二部分 Part 2

课文 Texts

一、热身 rèshēn Warm-up

1\. 给词语选择对应的图片。 Match the pictures with corresponding words.

A.

B.

C.

D.

wénběn ① 文本________ text	xuǎnzé ② 选择________ choice	liánjiēxiàn ③ 连接线________ connecting line	xíngzhuàng ④ 形状 ________ shape

2\. 观看介绍"亿图图示"软件界面的视频，将正确选项填入软件界面对应的位置。

Watch the video about the interface of the software EdrawMax, and fill the correct answers in the corresponding positions of the interface.

kuàijié càidān A. 快捷菜单 shortcut menu	fúhàokù B. 符号库 symbol library	xuǎnsèqū C. 选色区 color selection area	gōngjùlán D. 工具栏 toolbar

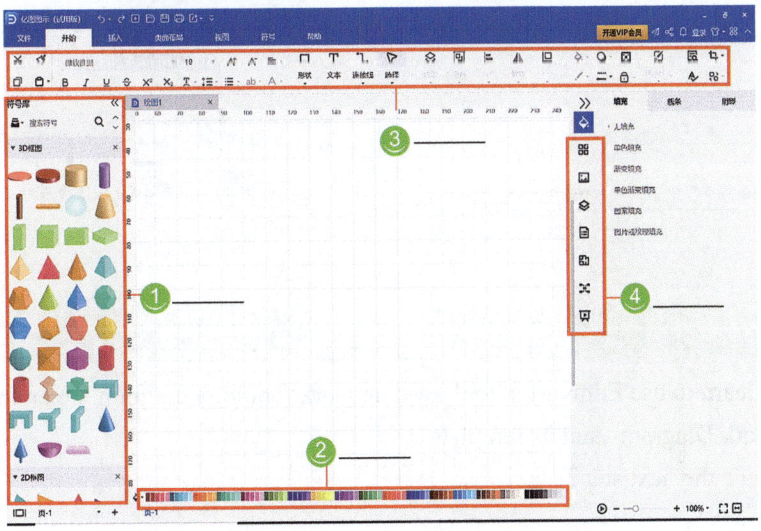

二、课文 kèwén Texts

A 09-01

shīfu: Jīntiān xuéxí shǐyòng "Yìtú Túshì" huà wǎngluò tuòpūtú. Dǎkāi ruǎnjiàn, xuǎnzé "wǎngluòtú" xuǎnxiàng hé múbǎn.
师傅：今天学习使用“亿图图示”画网络拓扑图。打开软件，选择“网络图”选项和模板。

túdì: Hǎo de. Xià yí bù rúhé cāozuò?
徒弟：好的。下一步如何操作？

shīfu: Shǔbiāo diǎnjī "chuàngjiàn" ànniǔ, xuǎnzé "múbǎn" hé shèbèi túbiāo. Zuìhòu, zài shèbèi zhījiān tiānjiā liánjiēxiàn.
师傅：鼠标点击“创建”按钮，选择“模板”和设备图标。最后，在设备之间添加连接线。

túdì: Hǎo de, wǒ lái shìshi. Xuǎnsèqū lǐ yǒu wǒ xǐhuan de hóngsè.
徒弟：好的，我来试试。选色区里有我喜欢的红色。

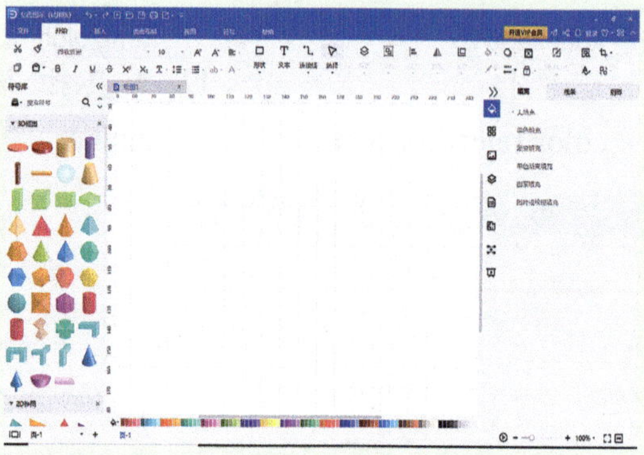

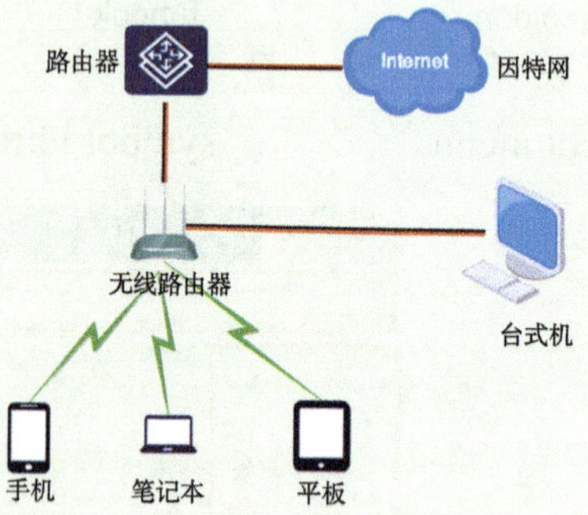

译文 yìwén Text in English

Master: Today, we'll learn to use EdrawMax to draw a network topology diagram. Open the software, and select "Network Diagram" and its template.

Apprentice: OK. What's the next step?

Master: Click the "Create" button with the mouse, and select the "Template" and device icons. Finally, add connecting lines between the devices.

Apprentice: OK. Let me have a try. There's my favorite color of red in the color selection area.

普通词语 pǔtōng cíyǔ General Vocabulary

09-02

1.	使用	shǐyòng	v.	use
2.	画	huà	v.	draw
3.	打开	dǎ//kāi	v.	open
4.	选择	xuǎnzé	v.	select, choose
5.	操作	cāozuò	v.	operate
6.	创建	chuàngjiàn	v.	create
7.	按钮	ànniǔ	n.	button
8.	最后	zuìhòu	n.	finally
9.	之间	zhījiān	n.	middle
10.	添加	tiānjiā	v.	add
11.	试试	shìshi	phr.	have a try
12.	里	lǐ	n.	inside
13.	喜欢	xǐhuan	v.	like
14.	红色	hóngsè	n.	red

专业词语 zhuānyè cíyǔ Specialized Vocabulary

09-03

1.	亿图图示	Yìtú Túshì	pn.	EdrawMax "a drawing tool"
2.	拓扑图	tuòpūtú	n.	topology diagram
3.	选项	xuǎnxiàng	n.	option
4.	模板	múbǎn	n.	template
5.	点击	diǎnjī	v.	click
6.	图标	túbiāo	n.	icon
7.	连接线	liánjiēxiàn	n.	connecting line
8.	选色区	xuǎnsèqū	n.	color selection area

B 09-04

túdì: Shīfu, chuàngjiàn hǎo de wǎngluò tuòpūtú, kěyǐ zài shǐyòng ma?
徒弟：师傅，创建好的网络拓扑图，可以再使用吗？

shīfu: Rúguǒ bǎocún tā, xià cì jiù kěyǐ zài shǐyòng.
师傅：如果保存它，下次就可以再使用。

túdì: Rúhé cāozuò?
徒弟：如何操作？

shīfu: Diǎnjī "bǎocún" ànniǔ, bìng xuǎnzé dǎochū wénjiàn géshi wéi ".eddx" de tuòpūtú.
师傅：点击“保存”按钮，并选择导出文件格式为“.eddx”的拓扑图。

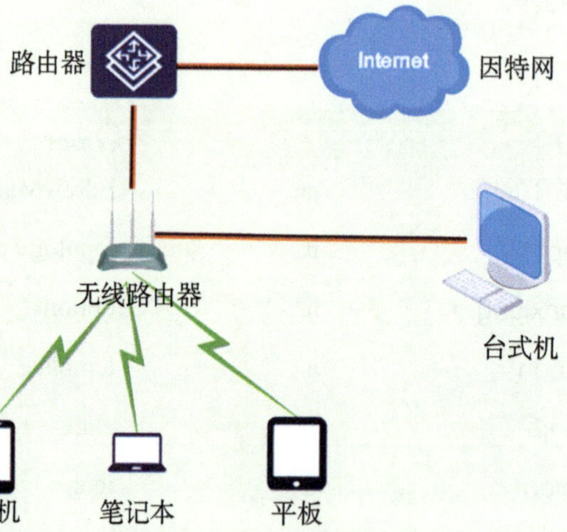

译文 yìwén Text in English

Apprentice: Master, can we use the finished network topology diagram again?
Master: Yes. It can be used again if we save it.
Apprentice: How do I save it?
Master: Click the "Save" button, and export the topology diagram in ".eddx" format.

普通词语 pǔtōng cíyǔ General Vocabulary

09-05

1.	再	zài	adv.	again
2.	下次	xià cì	phr.	next time

专业词语 zhuānyè cíyǔ Specialized Vocabulary

09-06

1.	保存	bǎocún	v.	save
2.	导出	dǎochū	phr.	export
3.	格式	géshi	n.	format

三、视听说 shì-tīng-shuō Viewing, Listening & Speaking

1. 观看介绍"亿图图示"的对话视频，把词语填入对应的横线，并模仿说出亿图图示的特点与内容。
Watch the video about EdrawMax, fill in the blanks with corresponding words, and speak out the characteristics and content of EdrawMax.

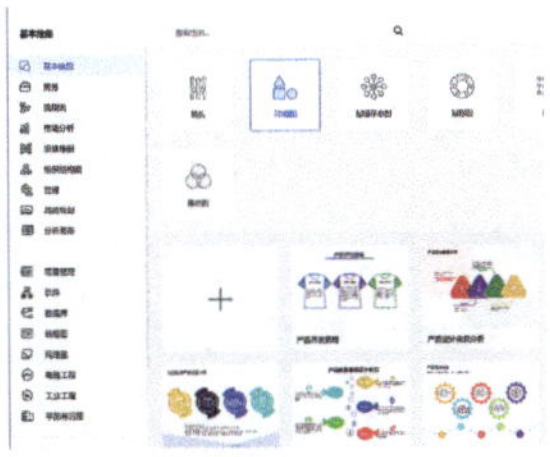

túbiǎo múbǎn
A. 图表模板
chart templates

Yìtú Túshì
B. 亿图图示
EdrawMax

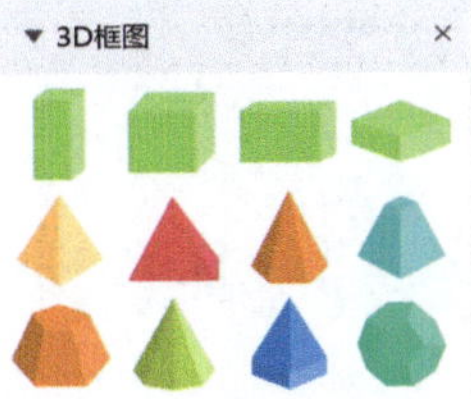

túbiǎo fúhào
C. 图表符号
chart symbols

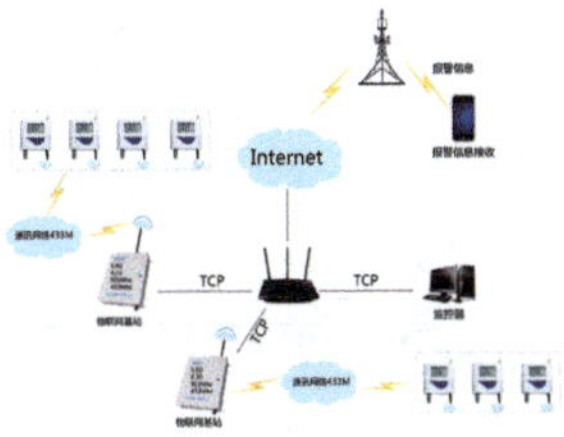

tuòpūtú
D. 拓扑图
topology diagram

Yìtú Túshì de tèdiǎn yǔ nèiróng
亿图图示的特点与内容
The characteristics and content of EdrawMax

tèdiǎn 特点 Characteristics	shì yì kuǎn huà ... de ruǎnjiàn, jièmiàn jiǎndān, cāozuò fāngbiàn. ① ______是一款画② ______的软件，界面简单，操作方便。 ______ is a software for drawing ______, which has a simple interface and is easy to use.
nèiróng 内容 Content	Yìtú Túshì bāohán fēngfù de ... yǐjí gè lèi 亿图图示包含丰富的③ ______以及各类④ ______。 EdrawMax contains abundant ______ and various ______.

2. 说一说　Let's talk.

请说出"亿图图示"的特点与内容。　Please speak out the characteristics and content of EdrawMax.

四、学以致用　xuéyǐzhìyòng　Practicing What You Have Learnt

观看介绍基本网络拓扑结构的视频，并将正确选项填在横线上。
Watch the video about basic network topological structures, and fill in the blanks with correct answers.

A. 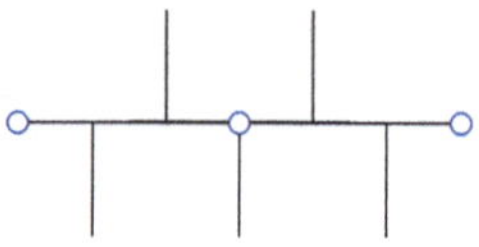

B. 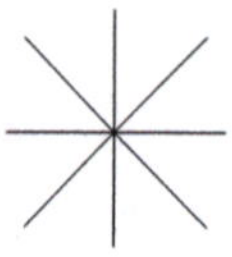

C. 

huánxíng tuòpū
① 环形拓扑 ______
ring topology

xīngxíng tuòpū
② 星形拓扑 ______
star topology

zǒngxiàn tuòpū
③ 总线拓扑 ______
bus topology

补充专业词语　bǔchōng zhuānyè cíyǔ　Supplementary Specialized Vocabulary　09-07

1.	文本	wénběn	n.	text
2.	形状	xíngzhuàng	n.	shape
3.	快捷菜单	kuàijié càidān	phr.	shortcut menu

4.	符号库	fúhàokù	n.	symbol library
5.	工具栏	gōngjùlán	n.	toolbar
6.	图表	túbiǎo	n.	chart, diagram
7.	界面	jièmiàn	n.	interface
8.	环形拓扑	huánxíng tuòpū	phr.	ring topology
9.	星形拓扑	xīngxíng tuòpū	phr.	star topology
10.	总线拓扑	zǒngxiàn tuòpū	phr.	bus topology

第三部分 Part 3

课堂用语 Classroom Expressions

1. 你昨天怎么没来上课？ Nǐ zuótiān zěnme méi lái shàngkè? Why were you absent from class yesterday?
2. 我期中考试没考好。 Wǒ qīzhōng kǎoshì méi kǎohǎo. I didn't do well in the mid-term exam.

第四部分 Part 4

单元实训 Unit Practical Training

绘制网络拓扑图 huìzhì wǎngluò tuòpūtú Drawing a Network Topology Diagram

实训目的 Training purpose

掌握使用“亿图图示”的方法和步骤，能够使用该软件画一个网络拓扑图。培养团队合作精神、竞争意识。

Master the methods and steps of using EdrawMax, and be able to use the software to draw a network topology diagram. Cultivate the spirit of teamwork and awareness of competition.

实训组织 Training organization

每组 3～5 人。选出一个组长。

Students work in groups of 3-5. Each group chooses a group leader.

实训内容 Training content

使用“亿图图示”画如图所示的网络拓扑图。

Using EdrawMax to draw the network topology diagram as shown below.

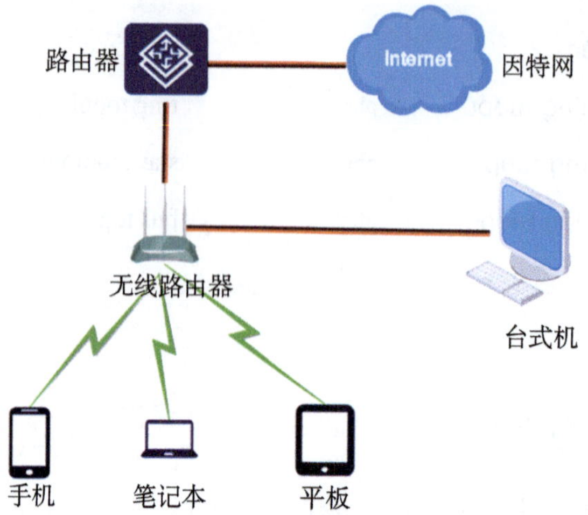

实训步骤 Training steps

1. 将参加实训的人员分成若干小组，每组 3～5 人。一人负责安装好亿图图示，第二个人将设备图标导入符号库，第三个人负责新建网络拓扑。接下来的步骤是：1）添加设备；2）在设备间添加连接线；3）保存拓扑图。

   Divide the students into groups of 3-5. One student is responsible for installing EdrawMax. The second student imports the device icons into the symbol library. The third student is responsible for creating a new network topology. The following steps are: 1) Add devices; 2) Add connecting lines between the devices; 3) Save the topology diagram.

2. 宣布比赛规则及要求：每组每人可以多次上机操作，安排专人记录每位同学操作所花费的时间，其他组同学监督。

   Announce the competition rules and requirements: Each member in each group can operate the computer for multiple times. A person who is specially assigned is responsible for recording the time each group member takes to operate the computer, and the members of other groups supervise the whole process.

3. 开始比赛。

   Start the competition.

4. 计算每组得分。

   Calculate the scores of each group.

5. 学员总结，教师总评。

   The students make a summary and the teacher comments on the training.

第五部分 Part 5

单元小结 Unit Summary

cíyǔ
词语
Vocabulary

普通词语 General Vocabulary

1.	使用	shǐyòng	v.	use
2.	画	huà	v.	draw
3.	打开	dǎ//kāi	v.	open
4.	选择	xuǎnzé	v.	select, choose
5.	操作	cāozuò	v.	operate
6.	创建	chuàngjiàn	v.	create
7.	按钮	ànniǔ	n.	button
8.	最后	zuìhòu	n.	finally
9.	之间	zhījiān	n.	middle
10.	添加	tiānjiā	v.	add
11.	试试	shìshi	phr.	have a try
12.	里	lǐ	n.	inside
13.	喜欢	xǐhuan	v.	like
14.	红色	hóngsè	n.	red
15.	再	zài	adv.	again
16.	下次	xià cì	phr.	next time

专业词语 Specialized Vocabulary

1.	亿图图示	Yìtú Túshì	pn.	EdrawMax "a drawing tool"
2.	拓扑图	tuòpūtú	n.	topology diagram
3.	选项	xuǎnxiàng	n.	option
4.	模板	múbǎn	n.	template
5.	点击	diǎnjī	v.	click
6.	图标	túbiāo	n.	icon
7.	连接线	liánjiēxiàn	n.	connecting line
8.	选色区	xuǎnsèqū	n.	color selection area
9.	保存	bǎocún	v.	save
10.	导出	dǎochū	phr.	export
11.	格式	géshi	n.	format

cíyǔ
词语
Vocabulary

补充专业词语 Supplementary Specialized Vocabulary

1.	文本	wénběn	n.	text
2.	形状	xíngzhuàng	n.	shape
3.	快捷菜单	kuàijié càidān	phr.	shortcut menu
4.	符号库	fúhàokù	n.	symbol library
5.	工具栏	gōngjùlán	n.	toolbar
6.	图表	túbiǎo	n.	chart, diagram
7.	界面	jièmiàn	n.	interface
8.	环形拓扑	huánxíng tuòpū	phr.	ring topology
9.	星形拓扑	xīngxíng tuòpū	phr.	star topology
10.	总线拓扑	zǒngxiàn tuòpū	phr.	bus topology

jùzi
句子
Sentences

1. 打开软件，选择“网络图”选项和模板。
2. 鼠标点击“创建”按钮，选择“模板”和设备图标。
3. 最后，在设备之间添加连接线。
4. 选色区里有我喜欢的红色。
5. 点击“保存”按钮，并选择导出文件格式为“.eddx”的拓扑图。

10

Wǎngluò fǎngzhēn

网络仿真

Network Simulation

wǎngluò móníqì de shǐyòng

网络模拟器的使用

Using a Network Simulator

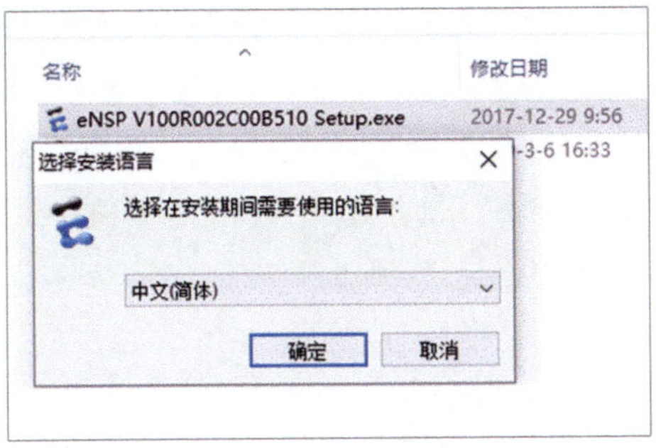

ānzhuāng wǎngluò móníqì ruǎnjiàn

安装 网络模拟器软件

install a network simulator software

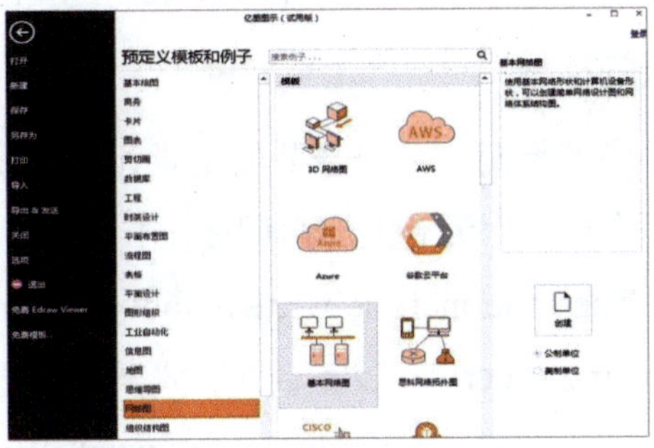

xīn jiàn wǎngluò tuòpū

新建 网络 拓扑

create a new network topology

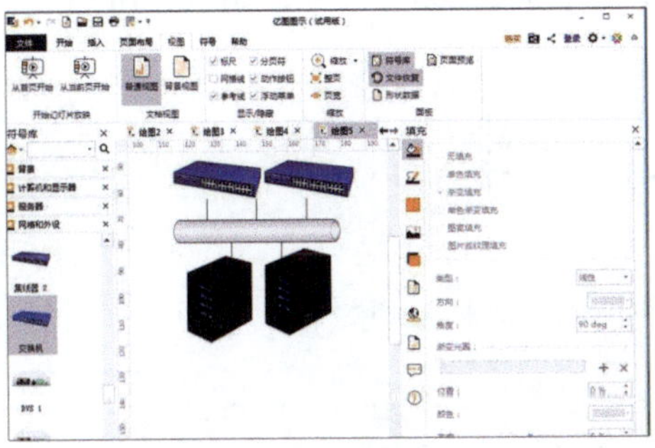

xuǎnzé shèbèi hé xiànlǎn, liánxiàn,

选择设备和线缆，连线，

zǔjiàn wǎngluò tuòpū

组建网络 拓扑

select the network devices and network cables, connect them and form the network topology

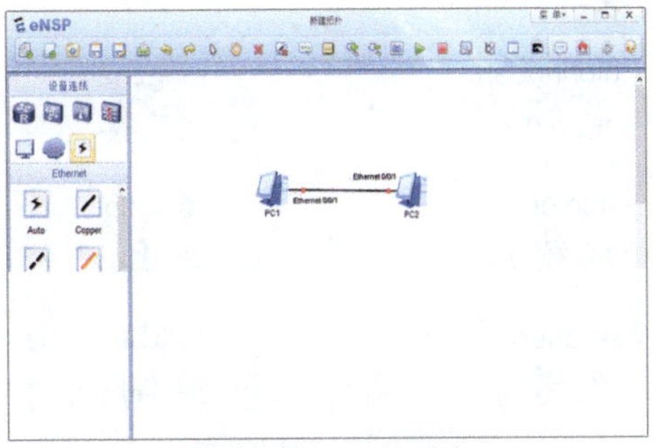

pèizhì bìng yànzhèng

配置 并 验证

configure and verify it

题解 Introduction

1. 学习内容：网络仿真的作用，网络模拟器的安装及网络仿真的步骤。
   Learning content: The functions of network simulation, the installation of a network simulator, and the process of network simulation.
2. 知识目标：掌握声调标写的基本规则，掌握与网络仿真相关的核心词语及表达。
   Knowledge target: Master the basic rules of tone markings; master the key words and expressions related to network simulation.
3. 技能目标：掌握安装和使用网络模拟器的基本方法和步骤。
   Skill target: Master the basic methods and processes of installing and using a network simulator.

第一部分 Part 1

语音 Phonetic Learning

一、语音知识 yǔyīn zhīshi Knowledge about Phonetics

声调的标写 Marking of tones

声调标写在一个音节的主要元音上，按照 a、o、e、i、u、ü 的先后顺序标调。韵母 iu、ui 的声调标在后一个元音上，声调标在 i 上面时，"i" 上的小点要省去。例如：

The tone mark is written above the main vowel of a syllable. The tone is marked according to the following order: "a", "o", "e", "i", "u", "ü". The exception is in the cases of "iu" and "ui", when the tone mark is written above the latter vowel. When the tone mark is placed on "i", the dot on the top of "i" is omitted. For example,

dà	mén	duō	lèi	xué	shuǐ	niú	xīn
大	门	多	累	学	水	牛	心

二、语音练习 yǔyīn liànxí Phonetic Exercises

读一读 Let's read.

① diànnǎoshì 电脑室	② fǎngzhēn 仿真	③ mónǐqì 模拟器	④ tuòpū 拓扑
⑤ xiànlǎn 线缆	⑥ liánxiàn 连线	⑦ zǔjiàn 组建	⑧ lèixíng 类型
⑨ xínghào 型号	⑩ huìzhì 绘制	⑪ fánghuǒqiáng 防火墙	⑫ qù 去

第二部分 Part 2

课文 Texts

一、热身 rèshēn Warm-up

1. 给词语选择对应的图片。 Match the pictures with corresponding words.

A.

B.

C.

D.

① xīn jiàn tuòpū
新建拓扑________
create a new topology

② huīfù shǔbiāo
恢复鼠标________
restore the mouse

③ kāiqǐ shèbèi
开启设备________
turn on the device

④ bǎocún
保存________
save

2. 观看介绍网络模拟器的视频，将正确选项填在横线上。
Watch the video about the network simulator, and fill in the blanks with correct answers.

A. gōngjùlán 工具栏 toolbar

B. shèbèi lèixíng 设备类型 device type

C. shèbèi xínghào 设备型号 device model

D. shèbèi xìnxī 设备信息 device information

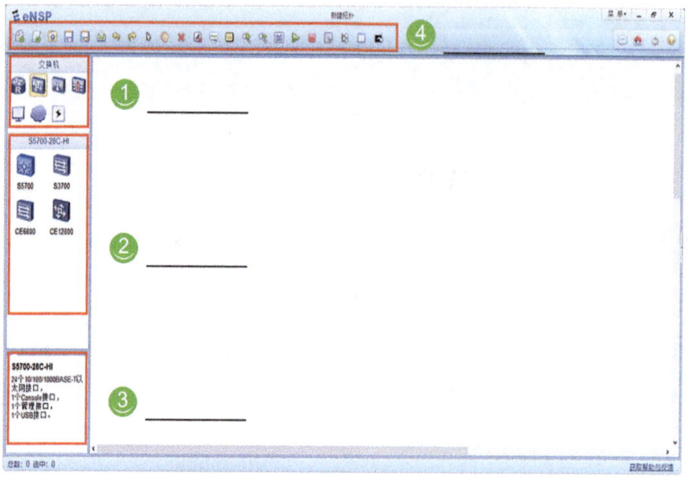

二、课文 kèwén Texts

A 10-01

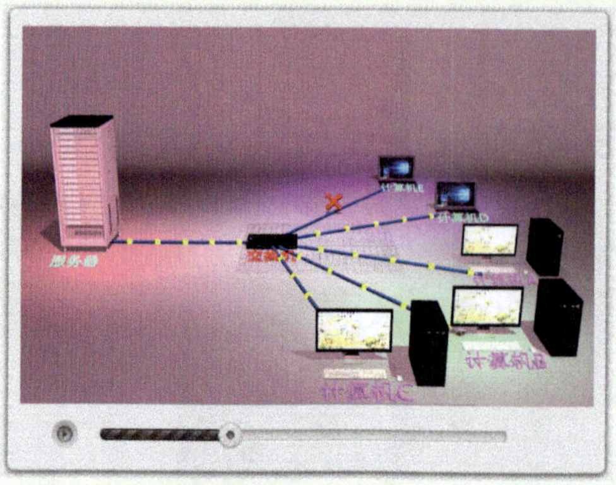

túdì: Qǐngwèn qù diànnǎoshì zěnme zǒu?
徒弟：请问 去电脑室怎么走？

shīfu: Yìzhí wǎng qián zǒu, zuìhòu nà jiān jiù shì diànnǎoshì.
师傅：一直 往 前 走，最后那间就是电脑室。

túdì: Hǎo de. Shīfu, shénme shì wǎngluò fǎngzhēn?
徒弟：好的。师傅，什么是网络 仿真？

shīfu: Wǎngluò fǎngzhēn shì yòng wǎngluò mónǐqì lái mónǐ wǎngluò yùnxíng.
师傅：网络 仿真 是用 网络 模拟器来模拟网络 运行。

túdì: Wǎngluò fǎngzhēn yǒu shénme yòng?
徒弟：网络 仿真 有 什么 用？

shīfu: Kěyǐ yònglái xuéxí wǎngluò zhīshi, yě kěyǐ yònglái yànzhèng wǎngluò pèizhì shìfǒu zhèngquè.
师傅：可以用来学习网络 知识，也可以用来 验证 网络配置是否 正确。

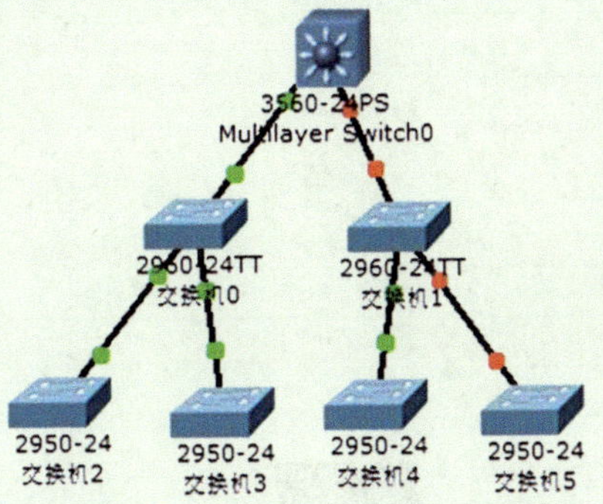

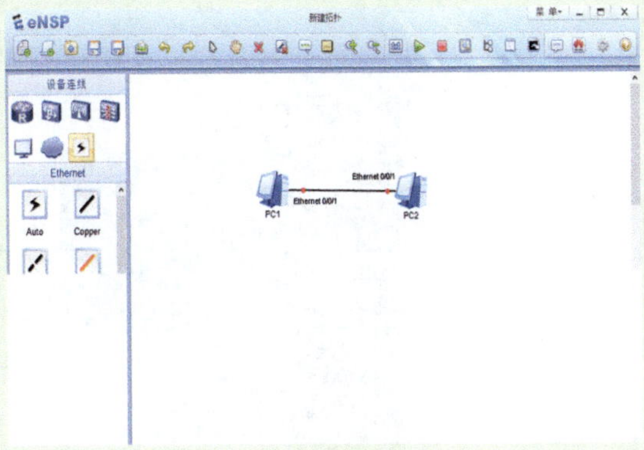

译文 yìwén Text in English

Apprentice: Could you tell me the way to the computer room?

Master: Go straight forward and the last room is the computer room.

Apprentice: OK. Master, what is network simulation?

Master: Network simulation is to simulate the network operation with a network simulator.

Apprentice: What is the function of network simulation?

Master: We can use it to learn the network knowledge, and verify whether the network configuration is correct.

普通词语 pǔtōng cíyǔ General Vocabulary

10-02

1.	去	qù	v.	go
2.	走	zǒu	v.	walk
3.	往	wǎng	prep.	toward
4.	前	qián	n.	front
5.	间	jiān	m.	*a measure word for rooms*
6.	模拟	mónǐ	v.	simulate
7.	运行	yùnxíng	v.	operate, run
8.	知识	zhīshi	n.	knowledge
9.	验证	yànzhèng	v.	verify
10.	配置	pèizhì	v.	configure

专业词语 zhuānyè cíyǔ Specialized Vocabulary

10-03

1.	电脑室	diànnǎoshì	n.	computer room
2.	仿真	fǎngzhēn	v.	simulate
3.	模拟器	mónǐqì	n.	simulator

B 10-04

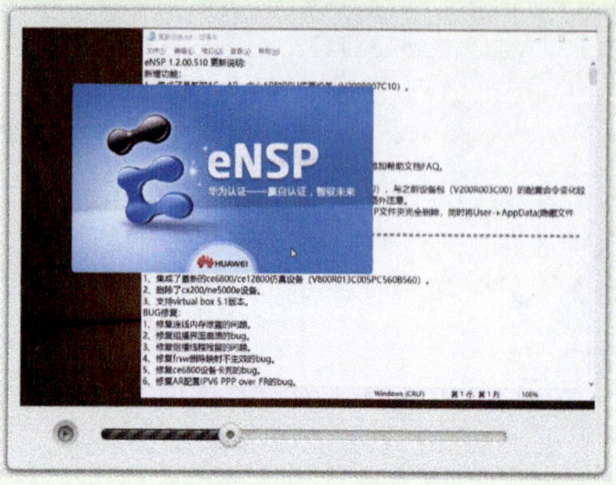

shīfu: Wǎngluò fǎngzhēn de dì-yī bù shì xiàzài bìng ānzhuāng wǎngluò fǎngzhēn mónǐqì. Dì-èr bù shì xīn jiàn tuòpū.
师傅：网络仿真的第一步是下载并安装网络仿真模拟器。第二步是新建拓扑。

túdì: Ránhòu ne?
徒弟：然后呢？

shīfu: Xuǎnzé xūyào de wǎngluò shèbèi hé wǎngluò xiànlǎn, liánxiàn, zǔjiàn wǎngluò tuòpū. Zuìhòu, pèizhì bìng yànzhèng.
师傅：选择需要的网络设备和网络线缆，连线，组建网络拓扑。最后，配置并验证。

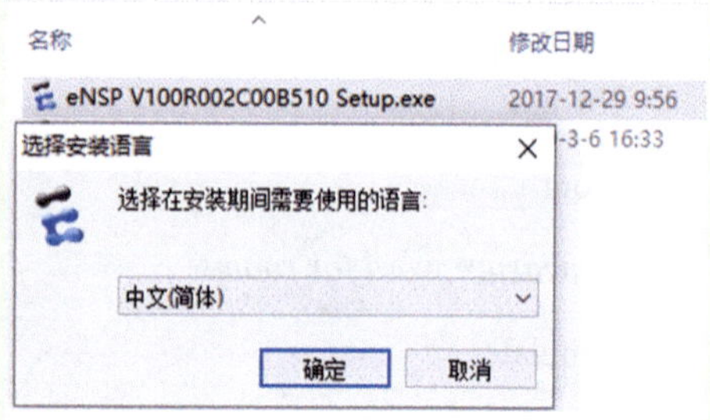

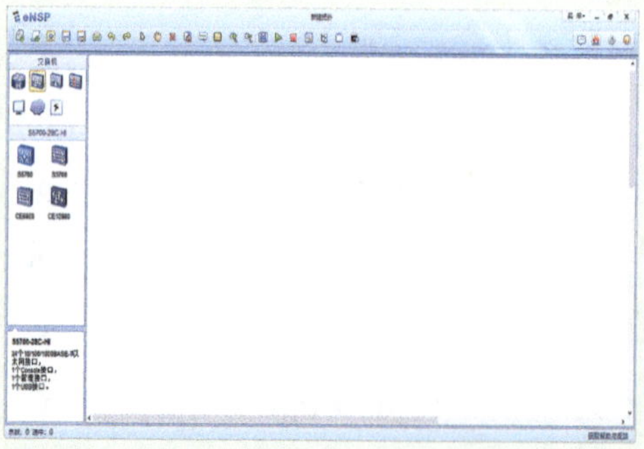

译文 yìwén Text in English

Master: The first step of making network simulation is to download and install a network simulator. The second step is to create a new topology.

Apprentice: What's next?

Master: Select the needed network equipment and network cables, connect them to form the network topology. Finally, configure and verify it.

普通词语 pǔtōng cíyǔ General Vocabulary

10-05

1.	新	xīn	adv.	newly
2.	建	jiàn	v.	create
3.	第二	dì-èr	num.	second
4.	然后	ránhòu	conj.	and

专业词语 zhuānyè cíyǔ Specialized Vocabulary

10-06

1.	拓扑	tuòpū	n.	topology
2.	线缆	xiànlǎn	n.	cable
3.	连线	liánxiàn	phr.	connect cables
4.	组建	zǔjiàn	v.	form

三、视听说 shì-tīng-shuō Viewing, Listening & Speaking

观看介绍用 eNSP 进行网络模拟的视频，按照先后顺序将下列操作步骤排序。

Watch the video about making the network simulation with eNSP, and put the following steps in the correct order.

1. huìzhì tuòpū 绘制拓扑 draw the topology diagram
2. xīn jiàn tuòpū 新建拓扑 create a new topology
3. bǎocún tuòpū 保存拓扑 save the topology
4. wǎngluò fǎngzhēn 网络 仿真 network simulation

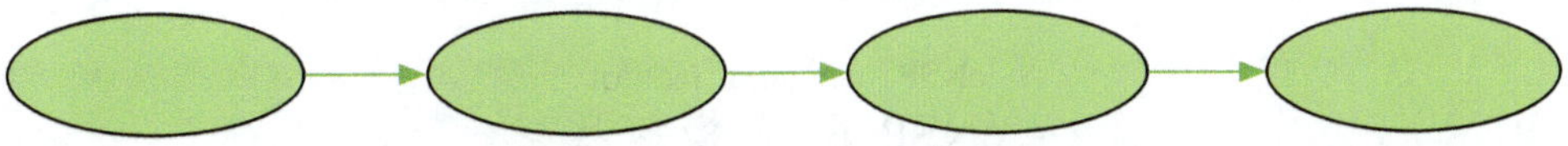

2. 说一说 Let's talk.

请模仿说出进行网络模拟的操作步骤。 **Please speak out the steps of making the network simulation.**

四、学以致用 xuéyǐzhìyòng Practicing What You Have Learnt

观看介绍 eNSP 网络模拟器的视频，将 eNSP 与其可以模拟的设备连线。

Watch the video about eNSP network simulator, and match the eNSP with the devices it can simulate.

lùyóuqì
① 路由器
router

jiāohuànjī
② 交换机
switch

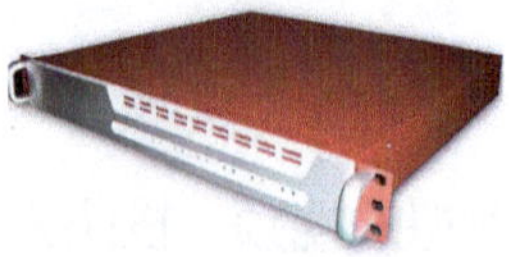

fánghuǒqiáng
③ 防火墙
firewall

wúxiàn júyùwǎng
④ 无线局域网
WLAN

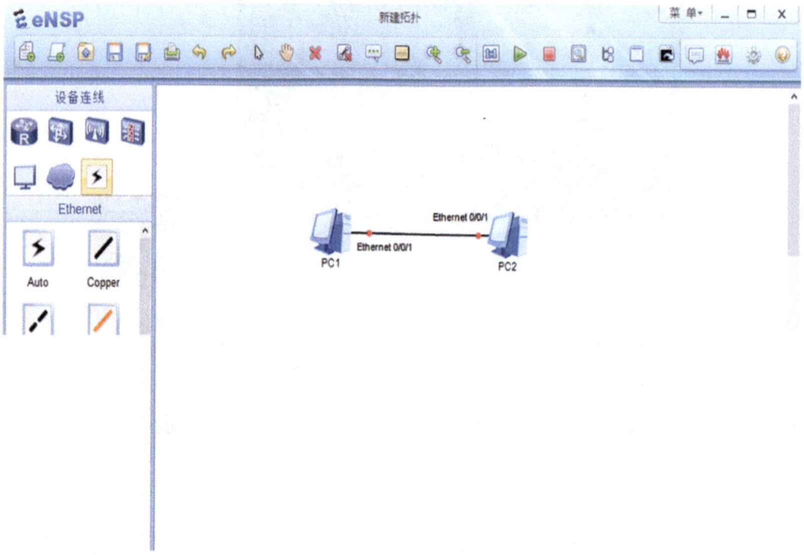

eNSP wǎngluò mónǐqì
eNSP 网络模拟器
eNSP network simulator

补充专业词语 bǔchōng zhuānyè cíyǔ Supplementary Specialized Vocabulary

10-07

1.	设备类型	shèbèi lèixíng	phr.	device type
2.	设备型号	shèbèi xínghào	phr.	device model

3.	设备信息	shèbèi xìnxī	phr.	device information
4.	绘制	huìzhì	v.	draw
5.	防火墙	fánghuǒqiáng	n.	firewall

第三部分 Part 3

课堂用语 Classroom Expressions

1. 十点上课，请大家准时。Shí diǎn shàngkè, qǐng dàjiā zhǔnshí. The class begins at 10 o'clock. Please be on time.
2. 现在听写。Xiànzài tīngxiě. Now it's time for dictation.

第四部分 Part 4

单元实训 Unit Practical Training

网络模拟器的使用 wǎngluò mónǐqì de shǐyòng Using a Network Simulator

实训目的 Training purpose

掌握安装和使用网络模拟器的基本方法和步骤，能够使用网络模拟器构建简单拓扑并实现网络模拟。培养团队合作精神、竞争意识。

Master the basic methods and steps of installing and using a network simulator, be able to use the network simulator to create simple topology and realize the network simulation, and cultivate the spirit of teamwork and awareness of competition.

实训组织 Training organization

每组 3 人。选出一个组长。

Students work in groups of 3. Each group chooses a group leader.

实训内容 Training content

安装并使用网络模拟器。

Installing and using a network simulator.

实训步骤 Training steps

① 将参加实训的人员分成若干小组，每组 3 人。每人轮流上机操作。1）安装网络模拟器软件；2）新建拓扑；3）选择需要的网络设备和网络线缆，连线，组建网络拓扑；4）配置并验证。

Divide the students into groups of 3, and all the group members take turns to operate the computer. 1) Install a network stimulator software; 2) Create a new topology; 3) Select the needed network equipment and network cables, connect them and form the network topology; 4) Configure and verify it.

② 宣布比赛规则及要求：每组每人可以多次上机操作，安排专人记录每位同学操作所花费的时间，其他组同学监督。

Announce the competition rules and requirements: Each member in each group can operate the computer for multiple times. A person who is specially assigned is responsible for recording the time each group member takes to operate on the computer, and the members of other groups supervise the whole process.

③ 开始比赛。

Start the competition.

④ 计算每组得分。

Calculate the scores of each group.

⑤ 实训结束，教师总结评价。

The teacher makes a summary and comment at the end of the training.

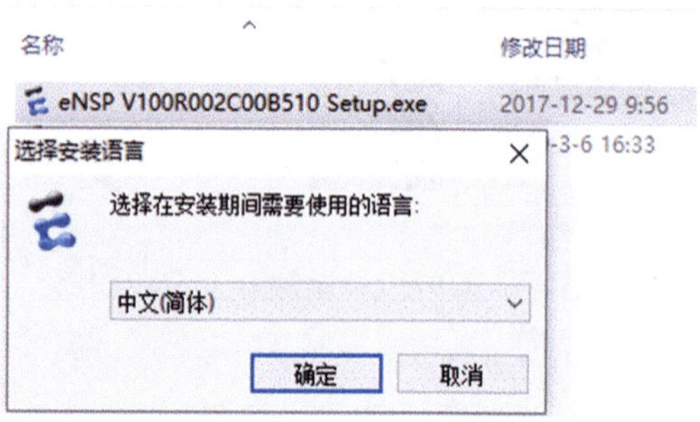

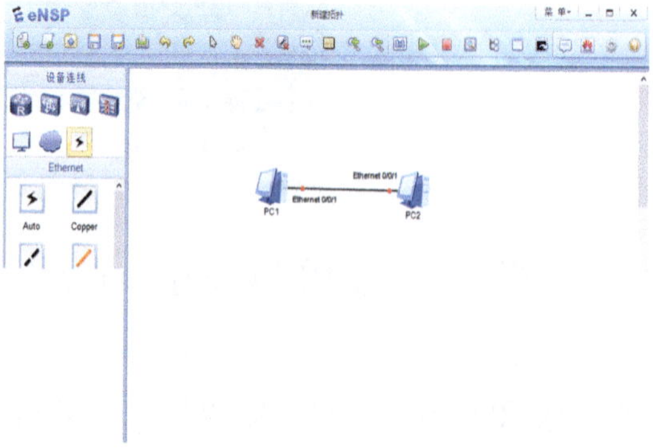

第五部分 Part 5

单元小结 Unit Summary

cíyǔ 词语 Vocabulary	普通词语 General Vocabulary			
	1. 去	qù	v.	go
	2. 走	zǒu	v.	walk
	3. 往	wǎng	prep.	toward
	4. 前	qián	n.	front

cíyǔ
词语
Vocabulary

5.	间	jiān	m.	*a measure word for rooms*
6.	模拟	mónǐ	v.	simulate
7.	运行	yùnxíng	v.	operate, run
8.	知识	zhīshi	n.	knowledge
9.	验证	yànzhèng	v.	verify
10.	配置	pèizhì	v.	configure
11.	新	xīn	adv.	newly
12.	建	jiàn	v.	create
13.	第二	dì-èr	num.	second
14.	然后	ránhòu	conj.	and

专业词语 Specialized Vocabulary

1.	电脑室	diànnǎoshì	n.	computer room
2.	仿真	fǎngzhēn	v.	simulate
3.	模拟器	mónǐqì	n.	simulator
4.	拓扑	tuòpū	n.	topology
5.	线缆	xiànlǎn	n.	cable
6.	连线	liánxiàn	phr.	connect cables
7.	组建	zǔjiàn	v.	form

补充专业词语 Supplementary Specialized Vocabulary

1.	设备类型	shèbèi lèixíng	phr.	device type
2.	设备型号	shèbèi xínghào	phr.	device model
3.	设备信息	shèbèi xìnxī	phr.	device information
4.	绘制	huìzhì	v.	draw
5.	防火墙	fánghuǒqiáng	n.	firewall

jùzi
句子
Sentences

1. 请问去电脑室怎么走？
2. 网络仿真是用网络模拟器来模拟网络运行。
3. 网络仿真可以用来学习网络知识，也可以用来验证网络配置是否正确。
4. 网络仿真的第一步是下载并安装网络仿真模拟器。
5. 网络仿真的第二步是新建拓扑。

附录 Appendix

词汇总表 Vocabulary

序号	生词	拼音	词性	词义	普通 G/专业 S	所属单元
1	A 类地址	A lèi dìzhǐ	phr.	Class A address	S	4B
2	安排	ānpái	n./v.	plan; arrange	G	6A
3	安装	ānzhuāng	v.	install	G	5A
4	安装包	ānzhuāngbāo	n.	installation package	S	6A
5	按钮	ànniǔ	n.	button	G	9A
6	B 类地址	B lèi dìzhǐ	phr.	Class B address	S	4B
7	把	bǎ	prep.	*used in the sentence pattern "Subject +* 把 *+ Object + Verb +..."*	G	5B
8	剥除	bāochú	phr.	strip	G	2B
9	剥线钳	bāoxiànqián	n.	wire strippers	S	2B
10	保存	bǎocún	v.	save	S	9B
11	笔记本	bǐjìběn	n.	laptop	S	1A
12	便捷	biànjié	adj.	convenient	S	1
13	并	bìng	conj.	and	G	5B
14	不	bù	adv.	not, no	G	7A
15	步	bù	n.	step	G	5B
16	部分	bùfen	n.	part	G	1B
17	C 类地址	C lèi dìzhǐ	phr.	Class C address	S	4B
18	材料	cáiliào	n.	material	G	5A
19	参数	cānshù	n.	parameter	S	8B
20	操作	cāozuò	v.	operate	G	9A
21	测试	cèshì	v.	test	G	2B
22	测试	cèshì	n.	test	S	8A
23	测线仪	cèxiànyí	n.	cable tester	S	2B
24	查看	chákàn	v.	view, examine, check	G	8A
25	常用	cháng yòng	phr.	common	G	4A
26	穿墙性	chuānqiángxìng	n.	penetrability	S	6
27	传播	chuánbō	v.	spread	G	3A
28	传输介质	chuánshū jièzhì	phr.	transmission medium	S	2
29	创建	chuàngjiàn	v.	create	G	9A
30	从	cóng	prep.	from	G	3B

（续表）

序号	生词	拼音	词性	词义	普通 G/ 专业 S	所属单元
31	打开	dǎ//kāi	v.	open	G	9A
32	带	dài	v.	carry with, be accompanied by	G	8B
33	单模光纤	dānmó guāngxiān	phr.	single-mode optical fiber	S	3A
34	导出	dǎochū	phr.	export	S	9B
35	到	dào	v.	get to	G	5B
36	得到	dé//dào	v.	get, obtain	G	7B
37	的	de	part.	*a modal particle used at the end of a sentence to indicate an affirmative tone*	G	2A
38	登录	dēnglù	v.	log in/onto	S	7
39	等	děng	part.	and so on, etc.	G	1B
40	第二	dì-èr	num.	second	G	10B
41	第一	dì-yī	num.	first	G	5B
42	第一步	dì-yī bù	phr.	first step	G	5B
43	点击	diǎnjī	v.	click	S	9A
44	电脑	diànnǎo	n.	computer	S	1A
45	电脑室	diànnǎoshì	n.	computer room	S	10A
46	电源线	diànyuánxiàn	n.	power cord	S	5B
47	掉线	diào//xiàn	v.	disconnect	S	7
48	对接	duìjiē	v.	butt-couple, splice	S	5
49	多	duō	adj.	many	G	3A
50	多模光纤	duōmó guāngxiān	phr.	multi-mode optical fiber	S	3A
51	多少	duōshao	pron.	how many, how much	G	4B
52	二维码	èrwéimǎ	n.	QR code	S	6B
53	范围	fànwéi	n.	range	G	4B
54	防火墙	fánghuǒqiáng	n.	firewall	S	9
55	仿真	fǎngzhēn	v.	simulate	S	10A
56	服务器网卡	fúwùqì wǎngkǎ	phr.	server NIC	S	1
57	符号库	fúhàokù	n.	symbol library	S	9
58	覆盖区域	fùgài qūyù	phr.	coverage area	S	6
59	高速	gāosù	adj.	high-speed	S	1
60	格式	géshi	n.	format	S	9B
61	工具栏	gōngjùlán	n.	toolbar	S	9
62	骨干级路由器	gǔgànjí lùyóuqì	phr.	backbone router	S	1

（续表）

序号	生词	拼音	词性	词义	普通 G/专业 S	所属单元
63	观察	guānchá	v.	observe	G	8B
64	管理员	guǎnlǐyuán	n.	administrator	G	7B
65	光	guāng	n.	light	S	3A
66	光口	guāngkǒu	n.	optical port	S	5B
67	光猫	guāngmāo	n.	optical modem	S	5A
68	光纤	guāngxiān	n.	optical fiber	S	3A
69	光纤模块	guāngxiān mókuài	phr.	fiber-optic module	S	3B
70	光纤跳线	guāngxiān tiàoxiàn	phr.	fiber-optic patch cord	S	3B
71	光纤网	guāngxiānwǎng	n.	optical fiber network	S	3B
72	广域网	guǎngyùwǎng	n.	wide area network	S	5
73	好	hǎo	adj.	well	G	5B
74	好的	hǎo de	phr.	OK, all right	G	8A
75	和	hé	conj.	and	G	1B
76	很	hěn	adv.	very	G	5A
77	红色	hóngsè	n.	red	G	9A
78	后	hòu	n.	back	G	8A
79	华为	Huáwéi	pn.	Huawei	G	6B
80	画	huà	v.	draw	G	9A
81	环形拓扑	huánxíng tuòpū	phr.	ring topology	S	9
82	绘制	huìzhì	v.	draw	S	10
83	IP 地址	IP dìzhǐ	phr.	IP address	S	4A
84	几	jǐ	pron.	several	G	4A
85	计算机	jìsuànjī	n.	computer	S	7A
86	间	jiān	m.	*a measure word for rooms*	G	10A
87	建	jiàn	v.	create	G	10B
88	键盘	jiànpán	n.	keyboard	S	1B
89	交叉线	jiāochāxiàn	n.	crossover cable	S	2
90	脚位	jiǎowèi	n.	Pin no	S	2
91	接入	jiērù	phr.	connect...to...	G	3B
92	接入级路由器	jiērùjí lùyóuqì	phr.	access router	S	1
93	接头	jiētóu	n.	connector	S	2A
94	结构	jiégòu	n.	structure	S	4
95	界面	jièmiàn	n.	interface	S	9

（续表）

序号	生词	拼音	词性	词义	普通 G/专业 S	所属单元
96	今天	jīntiān	n.	today	G	4B
97	就	jiù	adv.	just, exactly	G	6A
98	局域网	júyùwǎng	n.	local area network	S	4
99	距离	jùlí	n.	distance	S	3
100	看得见	kàndejiàn	v.	can be seen, be visible	G	6A
101	抗干扰性	kànggānrǎoxìng	n.	interference immunity	S	7
102	可以	kěyǐ	aux.	may, can	G	8A
103	快捷菜单	kuàijié càidān	phr.	shortcut menu	S	9
104	宽带	kuāndài	n.	broadband	S	5A
105	来	lái	v.	be here	G	8A
106	了	le	part.	*an aspect particle indicating a change of state*	G	7B
107	类	lèi	m.	type	G	4A
108	类型	lèixíng	n.	type	G	4A
109	冷	lěng	adj.	cold	G	7A
110	冷接子	lěngjiēzǐ	n.	cold connector	S	5A
111	里	lǐ	n.	inside	G	9A
112	里面	lǐmiàn	n.	inside	G	6A
113	连接	liánjiē	v.	connect	G	2A
114	连接线	liánjiēxiàn	n.	connecting line	S	9A
115	连通性	liántōngxìng	n.	connectivity	S	2B
116	连线	liánxiàn	phr.	connect cables	S	10B
117	联网	lián//wǎng	v.	be connected to the Internet	S	8B
118	两	liǎng	num.	two	G	8B
119	路径	lùjìng	n.	path	G	3A
120	吗	ma	part.	*used at the end of a yes/no question*	G	5A
121	忙	máng	adj.	busy	G	5A
122	密码	mìmǎ	n.	password	S	6
123	密钥	mìyào	n.	encryption key	S	7
124	命令	mìnglìng	n.	command	S	8A
125	摸得着	mōdezháo	phr.	can be touched, be tangible	G	6A
126	模拟	mónǐ	v.	simulate	G	10A
127	模拟器	mónǐqì	n.	simulator	S	10A

（续表）

序号	生词	拼音	词性	词义	普通 G/专业 S	所属单元
128	默认网关	mòrèn wǎngguān	phr.	default gateway	S	7B
129	模板	múbǎn	n.	template	S	9A
130	哪	nǎ	pron.	which	G	4A
131	哪些	nǎxiē	pron.	which ones	G	1B
132	那	nà	pron.	that	G	1A
133	那	nà	conj.	so, and	G	2B
134	呢	ne	part.	*used at the end of an interrogative sentence*	G	1B
135	能	néng	aux.	can	G	6A
136	能否	néngfǒu	v.	can or cannot	G	8B
137	你	nǐ	pron.	you	G	5A
138	ping 命令	ping mìnglìng	phr.	ping command	S	8B
139	配置	pèizhì	v.	configure	G	10A
140	企业级路由器	qǐyèjí lùyóuqì	phr.	enterprise router	S	1
141	前	qián	n.	front	G	10A
142	请问	qǐngwèn	v.	excuse me, may I ask	G	1B
143	区别	qūbié	n.	difference	G	3A
144	去	qù	v.	go	G	10A
145	RJ45 水晶头	RJ45 shuǐjīngtóu	phr.	RJ45 plug	S	2A
146	然后	ránhòu	conj.	and	G	10B
147	热	rè	adj.	hot	G	7A
148	如果	rúguǒ	conj.	if	G	8B
149	如何	rúhé	pron.	what way	G	5A
150	入户光纤	rùhù guāngxiān	phr.	in-building optical fiber	S	5B
151	软件	ruǎnjiàn	n.	software	S	6A
152	三	sān	num.	three	G	4A
153	扫描	sǎomiáo	v.	scan	S	6B
154	上网	shàng//wǎng	v.	get access to the Internet	S	7A
155	设备	shèbèi	n.	equipment	S	3B
156	设备类型	shèbèi lèixíng	phr.	device type	S	10
157	设备信息	shèbèi xìnxī	phr.	device information	S	10
158	设备型号	shèbèi xínghào	phr.	device model	S	10
159	设置	shèzhì	v.	set	S	4

（续表）

序号	生词	拼音	词性	词义	普通 G/专业 S	所属单元
160	什么	shénme	pron.	what	G	1A
161	生活	shēnghuó	n.	life	S	6B
162	师傅	shīfu	n.	master	S	1A
163	时候	shíhou	n.	time, moment	G	3B
164	使用	shǐyòng	v.	use	G	9A
165	试试	shìshi	phr.	have a try	G	9A
166	是	shì	v.	be	G	1A
167	是……的	shì…de	phr.	*a phrase used to categorize sth.*	G	2A
168	是否	shìfǒu	adv.	yes or no	G	8B
169	手机	shǒujī	n.	mobile phone	G	6A
170	首先	shǒuxiān	adv.	first of all	G	7A
171	输入	shūrù	v.	type in	S	8A
172	属性	shǔxìng	n.	property	S	4
173	鼠标	shǔbiāo	n.	mouse	S	1B
174	双绞线	shuāngjiǎoxiàn	n.	twisted pair	S	2B
175	搜索	sōusuǒ	v.	search	S	6
176	它	tā	pron.	it	G	8A
177	台	tái	m.	*a measure word for certain devices*	G	8B
178	台式	táishì	adj.	desktop	S	1A
179	提供	tígōng	v.	provide	G	7B
180	提示符	tíshìfú	n.	prompt	S	8A
181	体系	tǐxì	n.	system	S	4
182	天气	tiānqì	n.	weather	G	7A
183	添加	tiānjiā	v.	add	G	9A
184	条	tiáo	m.	*used to indicate paths, trousers, etc.*	G	3A
185	跳接线	tiào-jiēxiàn	n.	patch cord	S	3B
186	图标	túbiāo	n.	icon	S	9A
187	图表	túbiǎo	n.	chart, diagram	S	9
188	徒弟	túdì	n.	apprentice	S	1A
189	拓扑	tuòpū	n.	topology	S	10B
190	拓扑图	tuòpūtú	n.	topology diagram	S	9A
191	外皮	wài pí	phr.	outer sheath	G	2B

（续表）

序号	生词	拼音	词性	词义	普通 G/ 专业 S	所属单元
192	网络	wǎngluò	n.	network	S	2B
193	网速	wǎngsù	n.	network speed	S	8
194	网线	wǎngxiàn	n.	network cable	S	5A
195	往	wǎng	prep.	toward	G	10A
196	为	wéi	v.	be	G	4B
197	文本	wénběn	n.	text	S	9
198	稳定	wěndìng	adj.	stable	S	1
199	稳定性	wěndìngxìng	n.	stability	S	7
200	我	wǒ	pron.	I, me	G	5A
201	我们	wǒmen	pron.	we, us	G	4B
202	无线网卡	wúxiàn wǎngkǎ	phr.	wireless NIC	S	1
203	五	wǔ	num.	five	G	4A
204	喜欢	xǐhuan	v.	like	G	9A
205	下	xià	n.	next	G	5B
206	下次	xià cì	phr.	next time	G	9B
207	下一步	xià yí bù	phr.	next step	G	5B
208	下载	xiàzài	v.	download	S	6B
209	显示器	xiǎnshìqì	n.	monitor	S	1B
210	线缆	xiànlǎn	n.	cable	S	10B
211	想	xiǎng	aux.	want	G	7A
212	新	xīn	adv.	newly	G	10B
213	信号	xìnhào	n.	signal	S	5
214	信息	xìnxī	n.	information	S	7B
215	星形拓扑	xīngxíng tuòpū	phr.	star topology	S	9
216	形状	xíngzhuàng	n.	shape	S	9
217	需要	xūyào	aux.	need	G	3B
218	选色区	xuǎnsèqū	n.	color selection area	S	9A
219	选项	xuǎnxiàng	n.	option	S	9A
220	选择	xuǎnzé	v.	select, choose	G	9A
221	学习	xuéxí	v.	learn, study	G	4B
222	沿着	yánzhe	phr.	(be/go/travel) along	G	3A
223	掩码	yǎnmǎ	n.	mask	S	7B
224	验证	yànzhèng	v.	verify	G	10A

（续表）

序号	生词	拼音	词性	词义	普通 G/专业 S	所属单元
225	要	yào	aux.	be going to	G	5A
226	也	yě	adv.	also	G	7A
227	一	yī	num.	one	G	3A
228	一共	yígòng	adv.	altogether	G	4A
229	一直	yìzhí	adv.	all the time	G	8B
230	以后	yǐhòu	n.	subsequence	G	7B
231	以太网	yǐtàiwǎng	n.	Ethernet	S	4
232	一般	yìbān	adv.	usually, generally	G	1B
233	亿图图示	Yìtú Túshì	pn.	EdrawMax “a drawing tool”	S	9A
234	应该	yīnggāi	aux.	ought to	G	7A
235	硬件	yìngjiàn	n.	hardware	S	6A
236	用	yòng	prep.	with	G	5B
237	用	yòng	n.	use	G	8A
238	用来	yònglái	phr.	be used to/for	G	2A
239	用途	yòngtú	n.	use, application	G	2B
240	由	yóu	prep.	by	G	1B
241	有	yǒu	v.	have	G	2B
242	有线网卡	yǒuxiàn wǎngkǎ	phr.	wired NIC	S	1
243	运行	yùnxíng	v.	operate, run	G	10A
244	运行命令	yùnxíng mìnglìng	phr.	running command	S	8
245	再	zài	adv.	again	G	9B
246	在	zài	prep.	in	G	8A
247	怎么	zěnme	pron.	what about, in what way	G	7A
248	怎么办	zěnme bàn	phr.	what to do	G	7A
249	怎么样	zěnmeyàng	pron.	what about	G	7A
250	这	zhè	pron.	this	G	1A
251	这个	zhège	pron.	this	G	8A
252	这些	zhèxiē	pron.	these	G	2A
253	正确	zhèngquè	adj.	correct	G	7A
254	正在	zhèngzài	adv.	just	G	8A
255	之间	zhījiān	n.	middle	G	9A
256	知道	zhīdào	v.	know	G	5A
257	知识	zhīshi	n.	knowledge	G	10A

（续表）

序号	生词	拼音	词性	词义	普通 G/专业 S	所属单元
258	直径	zhíjìng	n.	diameter	S	3
259	直通线	zhítōngxiàn	n.	straight-through cable	S	2
260	智慧	zhìhuì	n.	wisdom, intelligence	S	6B
261	智慧生活	zhìhuì shēnghuó	phr.	AI Life	S	6B
262	中	zhōng	n.	middle, center	G	2A
263	种	zhǒng	m.	type, kind	G	4A
264	重要	zhòngyào	adj.	important	G	2A
265	主机	zhǔjī	n.	host	S	1B
266	转换	zhuǎnhuàn	v.	convert	S	5
267	子网	zǐwǎng	n.	subnet	S	7B
268	子网掩码	zǐwǎng yǎnmǎ	phr.	subnet mask	S	7B
269	自动连接	zìdòng liánjiē	phr.	auto connection	S	7
270	总线拓扑	zǒngxiàn tuòpū	phr.	bus topology	S	9
271	走	zǒu	v.	walk	G	10A
272	组成	zǔchéng	v.	consist of	G	1B
273	组建	zǔjiàn	v.	form	S	10B
274	最后	zuìhòu	n.	finally	G	9A
275	做	zuò	v.	do, make	G	2A

视频脚本 Video Scripts

第一单元 认识网络设备

一、热身

A：交换机有哪些类型？

B：根据交换机接口数目一般分为八口、十六口、二十四口、四十八口等多种，接口数目根据需求来选择。

三、视听说

A：你知道网卡一般有哪些类型吗？

B：我知道。网卡一般有有线网卡、无线网卡、服务器网卡等类型。

A：它们有什么区别吗？

B：有线网卡更稳定；无线网卡更便捷，可以随身携带使用；服务器网卡网速非常快。

四、学以致用

小机器人：大家好！路由器功能上可以划分为骨干级、企业级和接入级三种类型。骨干级路由器主要是实现企业级的网络互联，企业级路由器主要是连接企业局域网与互联网，接入级路由器主要连接家庭或者小型企业等。

单元实训 认识网络设备

小机器人：大家好！网络的运行需要电脑、交换机、路由器、网卡、服务器，让我们一起来看看它们之间是如何连接起来工作的吧！

第二单元 使用网线

一、热身

小机器人：RJ45 水晶头是双绞线的接头，测线仪用于测试网线的连通性，双绞线是常用的传输介质，剥线钳用于剥除双绞线的外皮。

三、视听说

A：你知道制作的网线分几类吗？

B：我知道。网线制作主要包括直通线与交叉线。

A：直通线与交叉线的作用是什么？

B：直通线用于异种设备的连接，而交叉线用于同种设备的连接。

四、学以致用

小机器人：今天我们学习怎样制作一根直通线。

1. 剥线。用剥线钳划开其外保护套，刀口距五类双绞线至少 2 厘米。
2. 排线。直通线两端的线芯均按照 T568B 标准进行导线颜色排线。即橙白色、橙色、绿白色、蓝色、蓝白色、绿色、棕白色、棕色。
3. 剪线。用压线钳剪断 8 根导线（剪平）。
4. 插线。一只手捏住水晶头，将有弹片的一侧向下，有针脚的一端指向远离自己的方向，另一只手捏平双绞线，最左边是第一脚，最右边是第八脚。
5. 压线。在确认一切无误后，将 RJ45 水晶头放入压线钳的压头槽内压实。
6. 测线。测试仪指示灯从 1 至 8 逐个按顺序闪亮，表明直通线制作成功。

单元实训 制作一根交叉线

小机器人：大家好！网线分为直通线和交叉线。今天我们来学习交叉线的制作。让我们一起来看看师傅是怎么制作的吧！

第三单元　使用光纤

一、热身

小机器人：首先，将一个光纤模块插入网络设备，然后将合适的光纤跳线插入光纤模块。本视频中使用的是单模光纤。

三、视听说

A：单模光纤有什么特点？

B：单模光纤护套皮的颜色通常为黄色，直径较小，传输距离较长，数据传输能力强。

A：多模光纤有什么特点？

B：多模光纤护套皮的颜色通常为橙色，直径较大，传输距离较短，数据传输能力不如单模光纤。

四、学以致用

徒弟：单模光纤一般适用于什么场景？

师傅：单模光纤一般适用于室外长距离。

徒弟：多模光纤一般适用于什么场景？

师傅：多模光纤一般适用于数据中心或建筑内部。

单元实训　光纤跳线的插接

小机器人：今天我们一起来学习光纤跳线的插接。通过认识光纤设备，了解光纤跳线如何接入光纤模块。我们跟着师傅一起来操作一下吧！

第四单元　网络地址

一、热身

小机器人：网络地址是怎么设置的呢？首先点击“网络”，右键点击“属性”，找到“网络和共享中心”；点击“网络和共享中心”，找到“以太网”；点击“以太网”，得到“以太网状态”；点击下方“属性”，找到“Internet 协议版本 4（TCP/IPv4）”；点击“Internet 协议版本 4（TCP/IPv4）”下方“属性”；进行 IP 设置。

三、视听说

徒弟：A 类地址适用于什么网络？

师傅：A 类地址适用于拥有大量主机的大型网络。

徒弟：B 类地址呢？

师傅：B 类地址适用于一般规模的中型网络。

徒弟：那 C 类地址是不是用于小规模的网络？

师傅：对，C 类地址适用于小规模的局域网络。

四、学以致用

徒弟：一般什么场所会使用大型网络？

师傅：大型网络一般用于像美国的苹果这类大型跨国公司。

徒弟：中型网络一般用于什么场所？

师傅：中型网络一般用于中等规模的公司和校园网。

徒弟：那局域网呢？

师傅：小型规模的局域网一般用于家庭网。

单元实训　静态 IP 地址的设置

小机器人：你知道静态 IP 地址是怎么设置的吗？让我们一起来学习一下吧。首先，鼠标右键点击“网络”，找到“属性”；点击“属性”，找到“以太网”；点击“以太网”，得到“以太网状态”，然后点击“详细信息”，在“详细信息”中，得到“IP 地址”；返回“以态网状态”，点击“属性”；点击“Internet 协议版本 4（TCP/IPV4）”，然后点击下方“属性”；在“属性”窗口中，选择“使用下面的 IP 地址”；将在“详细信息”中得到的“IP 地址”进行填写即可。

第五单元　宽带上网

一、热身

A：光纤、光猫和冷接子分别起什么作用？

B：光纤也叫光导纤维，用来传输光信号。光猫是光信号收发设备，起转换信号的作用。冷接子用于光纤对接光纤，相当于接头。

三、视听说

A：以太网和因特网有什么不同？

B：以太网是一种实现局域网的技术，也就是局限在一定的距离之内，只能连接附近的设备，我们可以有很多个以太网。而因特网是连接网络的网络，我们只有一个因特网。

四、学以致用

小机器人：你知道什么是局域网吗？局域网（LAN）是相对于广域网（WAN）而言，主要是指在小范围内的计算机互联网络。这个“小范围”可以是一个家庭，一所学校，一家公司，或者是一个政府部门。一般所涉及的地理范围最大不到 10 千米。局域网专用性非常强，比较稳定。

单元实训　安装宽带网络

小机器人：你知道怎么安装宽带网络吗？让我们跟师傅一起来学习一下吧。

第一步，将光猫连接到入户光纤，并连接好光猫的电源；第二步，将宽带路由器连接到光猫，并连接好宽带路由器的电源；第三步，检查光猫与宽带路由器的连接是否正确，等待光猫与宽带路由器的状态变为就绪；最后，对宽带路由器进行配置。

第六单元　组建无线网络

一、热身

小机器人：你知道如何安装华为“智慧生活”APP 吗？正确的流程是：

①打开华为“应用市场”APP；

②在搜索框中输入汉字“智慧生活”；

③点击“搜索”；

④找到“智慧生活”APP，点击“安装”按钮；

⑤点击“打开”按钮。

三、视听说

小机器人：大家好！你们知道无线网是怎么一回事了吗？Wi-Fi 不需要通过有线传输介质连接网络，而是通过无线电波来连接网络。WLAN（Wireless Local Area Networks）是一种无线局域网技术，可以使多个用户连接。只要是在它的覆盖区域内，就可以随时连接上网，非常方便，不需要顾虑流量的消耗，但必须知道密码哦！它的穿墙性比较弱。

四、学以致用

A：子母路由器是怎么工作的？

B：子母路由器是针对大中户型 Wi-Fi 覆盖的一整套解决方案。母路由器负责客厅等大部分区域的 Wi-Fi 覆盖，子路由器用于扩展母路由器的 Wi-Fi，可一母带多子。

A：子路由器还需配置吗？

B：不用，子路由器即插即用。它可自动学习母路由的 Wi-Fi 配置，无需用户再配置，覆盖能力不凡。

单元实训　配置无线网络

小机器人：你知道怎么安装子母路由器吗？让我们跟师傅一起来学习一下吧。

徒弟：子母路由器如何安装？

师傅：首先，准备好硬件：子母路由器、网线、电源线、手机。

徒弟：准备好了，也已经连接好了。然后怎么办？

师傅：准备安装软件。首先，打开“应用市场”，安装“智慧生活”APP；然后，点击“配置”按钮，进行手机端的配置。

徒弟：在电脑上也可以安装和配置吗？

师傅：是的。

第七单元　计算机上网设置

一、热身

A：请问计算机的 IP 地址是怎么一回事？

B：根据 IP（Internet Protocol）协议，给因特网上的每台计算机都规定了一个唯一的地址，叫“IP 地址”。IP 地址被用来给 Internet 上的电脑一个编号。如果把个人电脑比作一台电话，那么 IP 地址就相当于电话号码。

三、视听说

A：有线网络和无线网络有什么不同？

B：有线网络需要网线，一般只可在固定点使用；而无线网络不使用网线，直接搜索连接 Wi-Fi 就行，可在一定范围内灵活使用。有线网络稳定性强，抗干扰能力强；而无线网络抗干扰性较弱，可能会出现掉线现象。

四、学以致用

A：计算机如何使用无线网络上网？

小机器人：第一步，点击屏幕右下方的两个图标（或）中的一个；第二步，点击无线网络名称；第三步，点击“自动连接☑自动连接”；第四步，点击“连接连接”；第五步；输入密钥（）。

A：为什么要关掉“自动连接”呢？

小机器人：因为电脑在日常生活和工作中起着很重要的作用，会保存着很多重要的个人信息和相关的工作信息，所以为了安全，你最好把电脑设置的自动连接网络关掉，使用密码登录。

单元实训　获取动态 IP 地址

小机器人：你知道怎么用计算机有线上网吗？让我们跟师傅一起来学习一下吧。

师傅：第一步，用网线把路由器的 WAN 口接到 Internet 端口，并用网线把交换机端口接入路由器的 LAN 口；第二步，用网线把计算机的 RJ-45 口接到交换机端口，观察路由器的灯是否亮，交换机的灯是否亮，并观察计算机网卡的灯是否亮；第三步，设置自动获得 IP 地址、自动获得 DNS 服务器地址；最后，打开浏览器，输入一个网址，看是否能上网。

第八单元　网络测试

一、热身

徒弟：师傅，网络测试的主要工作有哪些？

师傅：主要包括：查看主机的 IP 地址，查看主机的计算机名，测试电脑能否上网，查看两台电脑能否联网等。

徒弟：可以查看电脑的价格吗？

师傅：这个不可以。

三、视听说

徒弟：师傅，如何测试计算机是否能上网？

师傅：共有四个步骤。
徒弟：第一步是什么？
师傅：第一步，使用 ipconfig 命令，得到计算机的 IP 地址、默认网关地址。
徒弟：好的，那第二步呢？
师傅：第二步，使用 ping 命令，ping 计算机自己的 IP 地址。
徒弟：然后呢？
师傅：第三步，使用 ping 命令，ping 默认网关地址。
徒弟：最后一步是什么？
师傅：第四步，ping 某一个网址。
徒弟：明白了。谢谢师傅！

四、学以致用

徒弟：师傅，网络测试的这几种命令都分别有什么用途？
师傅：运用运行命令可以打开命令程序界面；ipconfig 命令可以查看主机的 IP 地址，可以查看计算机名等。
徒弟：ping 命令有哪些用途？
师傅：ping 命令的用途包括查看电脑是否连网等。
徒弟：带参数 -t 的 ping 命令呢？
师傅：带参数 -t 的 ping 命令可以用来测试网络的稳定性等。
徒弟：明白了。谢谢师傅！

单元实训　使用网络测试命令

小机器人：大家好！我们一起来练习 ipconfig 和 ping 命令的使用。第一步，在计算机 PC1 运行 cmd 命令；第二步，输入 ping 210.28.101.100；第三步，当出现下图，来自 210.28.101.100 的回复：字节 =32 时间 <1ms TTL=128，表示 PC1 和 PC2 是联网的。

第九单元　绘制网络拓扑图

一、热身

徒弟：师傅，您好！“亿图图示”软件是用来干什么的？
师傅：可以使用“亿图图示”软件画网络拓扑图。
徒弟：“亿图图示”软件界面有哪几个部分？
师傅：你看，“亿图图示”软件界面主要有符号库、选色区、快捷菜单和工具栏这四个部分。
徒弟：看到了。谢谢师傅！

三、视听说

徒弟：师傅，亿图图示软件有什么特点？
师傅：亿图图示是一款适合新手的入门级的画拓扑图的软件，界面简单，操作方便。
徒弟：它包含哪些内容？
师傅：它有丰富的图表符号以及各类图表模板。
徒弟：知道了。谢谢师傅！

四、学以致用

徒弟：师傅，请问有没有最基本的网络拓扑结构？
师傅：有的，有三种最基本的网络拓扑结构。
徒弟：哪三种？
师傅：主要有星形拓扑、环形拓扑和总线拓扑这三种。
徒弟：知道了。谢谢师傅！

单元实训　绘制网络拓扑图

小机器人：大家好！今天我们来操练使用“亿图图示”画网络拓扑图。第一步，安装好“亿图图示”；第二步，将设备图标导入符号库；第三步，新建网络拓扑；第四步，添加设备，然后在设备间添加连接线；最后，保存拓扑图。

第十单元　网络仿真

一、热身

徒弟：师傅，你好！网络模拟器软件是用来干什么的？

师傅：网络模拟器可以用来模拟网络运行，从而实现网络仿真。

徒弟：网络模拟器软件界面有哪几个部分？

师傅：你看，网络模拟器界面主要有设备类型、设备型号、设备信息和工具栏这四个部分。

三、视听说

徒弟：师傅，如何用 eNSP 进行网络模拟？

师傅：共有四个步骤。首先，点击新建拓扑。

徒弟：然后呢？

师傅：第二步，绘制拓扑；第三步，网络仿真。

徒弟：好的，师傅！下面呢？

师傅：最后，保存拓扑并关闭模拟器。

徒弟：知道了。谢谢师傅！

四、学以致用

徒弟：eNSP 是网络模拟器吗？

师傅：是的，它是华为公司推出的一款强大的图形化网络模拟工具平台。

徒弟：eNSP 模拟器有什么功能？

师傅：它能够对企业网路由器、交换机、防火墙、WLAN 等设备进行软件模拟。它能呈现真实设备部署实景，让你有机会在没有真实设备的情况下也能够开展实验测试、学习网络技术。

单元实训　网络模拟器的使用

小机器人：今天我们操练安装并使用网络模拟器。主要有四个步骤：第一步，安装网络模拟器软件；第二步，新建拓扑；第三步，选择需要的网络设备和网络线缆，连线，组建网络拓扑；最后，配置并验证。

参考答案 Keys

第一单元 认识网络设备

一、热身

1. ①C ②B ③A ④D
2. ①B ②C ③A ④D

三、视听说

①A ②C ③B

四、学以致用

①BE ②CD ③A

第二单元 使用网线

一、热身

1. ①D ②C ③B ④A
2. RJ45 水晶头—连接；测线仪—测试；双绞线—传输；剥线钳—剥除

三、视听说

①A ②B

四、学以致用

1. D 2. A 3. C 4. B 5. F 6. H 7. G 8. E

第三单元 使用光纤

一、热身

1. ①A ②D ③C ④B
2. ①B ②C ③A ④D

三、视听说

① ADF ② BCE

四、学以致用

①BD ②AC

第四单元 网络地址

一、热身

1. ①C ②B ③A ④D
2. ①C ②B ③D ④A

三、视听说

①C ②A ③B

四、学以致用

①C ②B ③A

第五单元　宽带上网

一、热身

1. ①A　②D　③B　④C
2. ①B　②C　③A

三、视听说

C D

五、学以致用

A B C G H

第六单元　组建无线网络

一、热身

1. ①D　②A　③C　④B
2. ①B　②E　③C　④D　⑤A

三、视听说

A B C D E

四、学以致用

①B　②A

第七单元　计算机上网设置

一、热身

1. A　2. C

三、视听说

①B C F　②A D E

四、学以致用

A D

第八单元　网络测试

一、热身

1. ①C　②A　③B　④D
2. B、D、E、F

三、视听说

A　D　B　C

四、学以致用

①——B；②——A；③——C；④——C、E

第九单元　绘制网络拓扑图

一、热身

1. ①B　②D　③C　④A
2. ①B　②C　③A　④D

三、视听说

①B ②D ③C ④A

四、学以致用

①B ②C ③A

第十单元 网络仿真

一、热身

1. ①A ②C ③B ④D

2. ①B ②C ③D ④A

三、视听说

②→①→④→③

四、学以致用

eNSP 网络模拟器 —— ①

eNSP 网络模拟器 —— ②

eNSP 网络模拟器 —— ③

eNSP 网络模拟器 —— ④